Do you ever long to re
simple life? That's what
World is all about. I have
and know from her lifestyle that she not only walks the
walk, but she talks the talk. She is a genuine woman of
God, and I highly endorse this book. Inez talks about
her life, her journey, and her faith in God. Her simple
stories are filled with truth and encouragement. For
best results, you need to take this book and read it by
a cozy fireplace or find a beautiful place in the woods.
I'm sure your faith will increase and you'll value life
more after reading this wonderful book.

—DALE GENTRY
Breakout Prayer Network

Inez, thank you for taking the time and sharing with
me and the world these great life experiences with a
level of honesty and practicality that is rare to find
in the world today. I found your book to be very easy
to read, with a tremendous amount of insight for all
believers, regardless of where he or she is in their walk
with the Lord. I believe this will be a great tool for the
Lord to work in people's lives. Thank you and God
bless you.

—DAN GRIFFIN
Co-owner, Red Rock Energy Partners, Ltd.

I have known Inez since 1989. She is one of the godliest
women that I have ever met. There is always a smile and
laughter coming from her, regardless of her circumstances. The description of older women in Titus 2:3–5
describes Inez. There is a maturity and strength in her
that can be drawn from. She has chosen to press in
toward the mark of the high calling in Jesus. In this
book, she begins with simple, almost childlike stories;

but hang on, because she moves with smoothness into the meatier things of God and takes you on a journey of truly learning to grow to maturity in the faith. This is a must-read.

—MIKE NELSON
President, Red Rock Ministries

I am happy to recommend to you Inez Alexander's uplifting collection of biblical and personal stories, *Walking the Walk in a Real World*. Inez has truly "walked the walk" of a devoted follower of Jesus for many years. She shares what she has learned in the crucible of life as His joyful disciple. The section on heroic women of God will inspire you, and her keen observations will give you godly, seasoned counsel. You will receive insight, strength, and fresh faith to "walk it out" in these encouraging pages.

—DAVID SHIBLEY
President, Global Advance

WALKING
THE WALK
IN A REAL WORLD

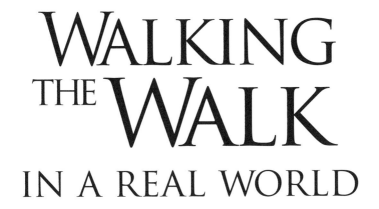

WALKING THE WALK

IN A REAL WORLD

INEZ ALEXANDER

CREATION
HOUSE
A STRANG COMPANY

WALKING THE WALK IN A REAL WORLD by Inez Alexander
Published by Creation House
A Strang Company
600 Rinehart Road
Lake Mary, Florida 32746
www.creationhouse.com

Unless otherwise noted, all Scripture quotations are from The Living Bible. Copyright © 1971. Used by permission of Tyndale House Publishers, Inc., Wheaton, IL 60189. All rights reserved.

Scripture quotations marked KJV are from the King James Version of the Bible.

Scripture quotations marked NKJV are from the New King James Version of the Bible. Copyright © 1979, 1980, 1982 by Thomas Nelson, Inc., publishers. Used by permission.

Cover design by Marvin Eans

Library of Congress Control Number: 2007934644
International Standard Book Number: 978-1-59979-256-9

First Edition

08 09 10 11 12 — 9 8 7 6 5 4 3 2 1
Printed in the United States of America

ACKNOWLEDGMENTS

I WOULD LIKE TO THANK MY CHILDREN AND GRANDCHILDREN for the joy they have brought to me all these years, and for allowing me to use their stories in my book, *Walking the Walk in a Real World.*

I would also like to thank my husband, Robert Alexander, for his statements, quotes, and for his love and spiritual input in my life as we commit together in walking our walk in a real world.

The Lord bless you and keep you; The Lord make His face shine upon you, And be gracious to you; The Lord lift up His countenance upon you, And give you peace.

—Numbers 6:24–26, NKJV

CONTENTS

INTRODUCTION

MANY TIMES WITH ALL SINCERITY, YOU MAY SAY THINGS like, "Lord, change my heart," or "Lord, when people look at me, I don't want them to see me; I want them to see Jesus and His love shining through me."

As I have grown in my relationship with the Lord, I have learned that you don't become like Jesus just because with a pure heart, you desire it. There are changes and a purging of attitudes and the heart that have to take place to become more like Jesus. You may have to deal with confusion, bitterness, anger, rebellion, self-pity, forgiveness, sorrow, disappointment, or your love relationships. But there is also laughter, joy, and the profound knowledge that you have a heavenly Father that loves and cares about you.

Through the years I have written a few things that I have learned as I have grown and developed in my relationship with the Lord. In this little book, I share a few of those experiences with you. I hope they minister to you and bring revelation, hope, and peace to your life as you walk your walk in a real world.

/

Chapter 1

FUN AND LAUGHTER

MERRY HEART

A merry heart does good, like medicine.
—Proverbs 17:22, NKJV

A FEW YEARS AGO I WORKED WITH FOUR-YEAR-OLD children. As part of our curriculum, we taught the children where food comes from; milk and beef come from cows, eggs from chickens, and so forth. As another way to teach this, at lunch we would discuss what we were eating and what animal or vegetable it came from.

One day we were going to have out-of-town visitors. I knew if they came during lunch, they would ask the children what they were eating. So when the meal, which was vegetable beef soup, was served, I discussed the meal and what we were eating. Just as I thought, after the children were served, the visitors came. They mingled among the children, talking and visiting with them. One man came to a little boy and asked, "What are you eating?" He thought for a second, and then yelled, "Cow Soup!"

My daughter-in-law was cooking one evening. Her son asked, "Mom, what's for dinner?" She said, "Goulash." Later when he was eating he said, "Mom, can I have some more *hog wash*?"

When I was pregnant with my first child, they were building a road from the city where we lived to the city where the hospital was located. We could go another way, but it was much farther. The road under construction was finished enough so that we could travel on it to the hospital. I gave birth to a beautiful baby boy, and the day arrived for us to take our little bundle of joy home. We decided to take the shortcut on the road under construction. Since the road was a new road, it was in an undeveloped area with trees all along both sides of the road. A unique thing happened: right in front of our path, a mama alligator and several baby alligators were on all four feet, walking across the road from one side to the other side. This may not spark laughter to a "merry heart," but it was very unusual for me and very interesting.

While living in the country, I was by myself driving to town one day. We had a car with stick shift; the gears were on the floor between the seats. I looked down at the gears, and a little mouse was sitting there on the gear mound. I started screaming, then realized what I was doing and started laughing. If anyone in the other cars saw me, I wonder what they were thinking. I think the mouse was just as startled as I was. I couldn't go anywhere, but he quickly disappeared.

My husband was in law enforcement for several years. He had to take his turn working the midnight shift, so he would try to sleep a little before going to work. We lived in a house with a screened Florida room, or sun room, on the side of the house off from the kitchen area and at the end of the carport. It was a nice night, so he took a nap in the Florida room. We had small children, so I decided to visit my mom while he slept. I came home a little before he had to wake up. Not wanting to wake him before he had to get up, as I drove into the carport I turned off the car lights. I misjudged my distance and ran into the support post near where he was sleeping. I wasn't looking forward to having to confess to my husband what I had done, but, needless to say, he knew before I told him!

When our boys were really young, they shared a bedroom. We were living in the country, and at that time, we didn't have central air conditioning. My husband was working the night shift, and since he had to sleep in the daytime, we installed a window air conditioner in the bedroom. It rained one night, and before my husband left for work, we went into the boy's room to check on them. To our amazement, frogs were making such a racket—croaking after the rain had stopped—we were surprised that they had endured all that noise. The next day my husband bought and installed a window air conditioner in their room. The hum of the air conditioner and closing the windows shut out the noise of the frogs.

When my husband was a teenager, he had a friend whose dad had an English bulldog named Bosco. He also had a restored Model T truck that had spoke wheels with skinny tires. His dad would let them use the truck to joyride. Every time they took off from the house in that truck, his friend would have to drive as fast as it could go to get away from the dog. When Bosco heard the truck running, here he came. He would chase the truck, and they would have to floorboard it to outdistance and get away from the dog, leaving him behind.

As most people know, English bulldogs have something about their jaws so that when they bite, their jaws lock and they can't let go. You have to work with them to get them to turn loose.

One day they had been off riding around in the truck, and they were coming home. As they approached the house, here came Bosco. He was really after that truck; he was gonna catch it. Since they were coming home rather than leaving, he was able to catch the truck and grabbed hold of the tire while it was going around. When he grabbed the tire and locked onto it, he couldn't turn loose and went round and round with the tire as the wheel turned. Bosco was having the fight of his life, but he finally caught that truck. They got the truck stopped, and in the process, the dog punctured a hole in the tire and caused it to go flat—but he still couldn't turn loose. They had to work with him to make him loosen his grip. Fortunately, it was a dirt road with loose, soft sand, so he wasn't harmed.

If you chase after trouble, be careful, you might catch it; and it may be a lot rougher ride and not as much fun as you thought it was going to be.

THE SKUNK

My husband grew up in Georgia on a bluff of a riverbank that flows into the Atlantic Ocean. There are large, beautiful oak trees on one side of the river and marsh grass on the other side. When he was a teenager, he loved to swim in the river and hunt among the oak trees and marsh grass.

He had a friend that loved to play pranks on people. One day while he was hunting, he saw this friend had parked his vehicle to hunt in the woods, too. Shortly after seeing the truck parked there, my husband came upon a skunk and killed it. In those days trucks had a running board that went from the front fender to the back fender to step up on to get into the truck. Thinking it would be funny to get back at his friend, he took the dead skunk back to the truck and laid it out on the truck running board to make it look like it was alive. Then he went on about his business of hunting and later in the day went home.

His friend came back to his truck and, seeing the skunk on his running board, thought the skunk was alive. Knowing the results if he moved him, he walked three or four miles home and left skunk and truck in the woods. The next day he went back to get his truck. The skunk was still sitting on it, so he realized it was a prank.

My husband didn't know for a long, long time what transpired when the man returned to his truck, and he didn't dare ask any questions. He didn't tell anyone until he was grown and married. All ended well!

On your travel down life's pathway, if you should find something stinky or ugly sitting on your running board, *be wise*; things aren't always what they seem.

Chapter 2

TALENTS, BLESSINGS, AND SAFETY

Flower in a Weed Patch

When you think you can handle life and life's situations by yourself and decide you don't need God, you may feel like a flower alone in a patch of weeds. God sends His rain and sunshine to make them grow beautiful. The little flower, because it feels a little independent and self-sufficient, might say, "I don't need your rain and sunshine." But, in order to live or survive, someone has to come along, show love, and water the little flower. God still provides the soil, rain, and sunshine. The flower continues to grow with the assistance of someone helping. God cares for the little flower, but the little flower might feel that he doesn't need His help.

God wants you to be bold and confident in Him, but He wants to be included in your life. He is your heavenly Father that loves you and wants you to have a good life full of His blessings. Seek Him, and let Him be a part of your decision-making and in every part of your life.

> We dare to say these good things about ourselves only
> because of our great trust in God through Christ, that he
> will help us to be true to what we say, and not because we

think we can do anything of lasting value by ourselves.
Our only power and success comes from God.

—2 Corinthians 3:4–5

When my oldest son was about five, we lived on a street where his grandparents lived behind us, house facing the next street, and a friend of his lived next door to them. On the way back home from his friend's house, there was an area with no grass that was sandy with sandspurs growing in the sand, and a single morning glory growing wild in a patch of weeds. My son wanted to pick the flower for me. If you step into the middle of the sandspur plant and are careful, you won't step on any spurs, but he didn't realize that the spurs were mixed all in the sand. He was barefoot, and when he stepped into the sand, the more he moved, the more sandspurs he got in his feet. His grandma heard him calling for help and, with shoes on, came and rescued him. He hung onto the flower, and gave it to me.

The flower was removed from the weeds, but someone still had to come and rescue my son. Sometimes you may get into a situation and feel that you are a flower alone in the middle of a prickly weed patch. There are spurs and thorns all around you that could affect you and get you into trouble if you try to handle life alone and unprepared. That is why you need God's protection to cover you. When you need Him, if you call on Him, in His loving mercy, He will come and rescue you and heal your wounds.

You are like a little flower blooming in the world. Jesus gave His life for you, so that you could have eternal life with Him. Do you love Him enough to deny yourself the desires of your heart and say, "Lord, I thank you for loving me, and I surrender my life to You this day and choose to walk in total submission to Your will for my life"?

You can never please God without faith, without depending on him. Anyone who wants to come to God must believe that there is a God and that he rewards those who sincerely look for him.

—Hebrews 11:6

GOOSE HOUSE

When my friend was a young girl, she had a goose named Ralf. Ralf was the neighborhood burglar alarm. They put a plastic kiddy pool in the back yard for him to swim in. He had no shelter from the sun and weather, so her dad decided Ralf needed a house. He built a shack with four walls, a roof, and a door. Her mother laughed at it. It was pretty primitive.

Now, many years later, her father is building beautiful log homes. Her mom can't believe he went from that funny-looking goose house to building beautiful homes.

Do not be afraid to use your talents; you have to start somewhere. As you learn, develop, and grow, you will then improve. One day, you will look back and see how far you have come, on your way to success!

In everything you do, put God first, and he will direct you and crown your efforts with success.

—Proverbs 3:6

SAFETY LEVEL

I was sitting in a Jacuzzi with a lady one day while the rest of the family was swimming or sitting around the pool next to the Jacuzzi. One of my granddaughters, who was very young at the time, was sitting between us. The lady was talking. All of a sudden, she picked up my granddaughter, threw her into the pool, and went right on chatting. In a matter of seconds,

I realized what happened and thought, "I don't know if she can swim!" I reached over the side of the Jacuzzi, and, as she was coming up, I pulled her out of the water. She was fine!

When you have been thrown into the deep waters of an unexpected experience or a position that you have not been trained or prepared for, you may find yourself treading water, not knowing how you got there. Don't despair, Jesus will reach down in His loving, watchful care and rescue you.

When you get out, you can either become afraid of the waters of life because of the experience, or you can look around and see life is still going on and you are safe. Then, instead of being thrown in over your head not realizing what happened, because it is your choice, you can forget the experience and jump into that same water at your level of safety and expertise—and have a great time!

GOOD THINGS

When one of my granddaughters was a year old, she loved ice cream. One day they were visiting grandma and grandpa, and we bought some ice cream. She would go around the room from one person to the other getting a bite. As soon as she would swallow that one bite, she went to someone else for another bite. It was really funny! She continued around the room until everyone's ice cream was gone. When there was none left in anyone's dish, she began to cry. She still loves ice cream to this day.

God has such wonderful, good things for you. He loves you and wants you to have His best. When you seek after Him with your whole heart, read the Bible, pray, worship, meditate on Him, and open yourself up to receive from Him, you can get into His holy presence.

The more you worship and love Him, the stronger you will feel His presence. He wants to love and comfort you, but He wants you to invite Him in and say, "Father, you are welcome in my life."

There will be times when you will want to ask Him for something, but first, love and worship and get into His presence, then ask for your needs to be met. He knows before you ask, but He loves you and wants your love in return.

> Oh, give thanks to the Lord, for he is good; his loving kindness continues forever.
>
> —Psalm 136:1

CHILDREN

Two of my grandchildren were living out of town when they were small. I sent them cards one time. I talked to my grandson about taking a walk with him when he came to visit. I talked to my granddaughter about learning to skip. A little later when they came for a visit, my granddaughter told me she had learned to skip. We went outside and held hands and skipped down the sidewalk together. My grandson remembered about going for a walk, so we went to a little area near the house and had a nice walk.

It is so important that you mean what you say and keep your promises to your children and grandchildren. Small, seemingly insignificant things mean a lot to them. They trust you and take what you say to heart. If they can trust you in the little things, when the bigger things come along, they know they can trust and depend on you.

You may think they won't remember the things you do, and you may not realize the importance of an action. Whether they remember the incident or not, you are building character. Then they will leave that same character-building legacy to the next generation. Their lives will be founded on what you have instilled in them: trust, love, hope, spiritual roots, family ties—all the foundational values you have taught them.

Give your children a foundation you will be proud of, love and guide them, and let them develop their own little personalities and characteristics. You will be so proud!

While you are proudly looking at your child and saying, "That's my child," God is lovingly looking at you and saying, "That's *My* child."

FAMILY

> Children are a gift from God; they are his reward. Children born to a young man are like sharp arrows to defend him. Happy is the man who has his quiver full of them.
>
> —Psalm 127:3–5

When I was a young girl before I was married, I would pray for my children and grandchildren; that they would be healthy and serve the Lord. God blessed me with three great sons and several beautiful grandchildren and great grandchildren. Now, I pray for their health, safety, and protection. God has brought us all through many situations.

One fall afternoon, my grandson and his family were visiting friends in another town. They had recently moved into another home and were remodeling. The three children were in the backyard playing. Their friend had been pulling up old floor tiles in the kitchen and had put them in a large garbage can. He put the can on a dolly to take out the back door to be hauled away. My grandson was sitting on the back porch near the door. They called to him to move so they could get through. He did not hear them, and the friend did not realize he had not moved. He was pulling the dolly backward out the door, and tripped over my grandson and fell. My grandson's face was cut, very near his left eye. It was very bad; it took eighteen stitches to sew it shut, and the scar is still there. It was bad, but it could have been much worse.

Pray daily for your family. Thank God for His salvation; His mercy and goodness; for keeping your family under the covering of His protection, health, safety; and for joy and blessings in their lives.

Pray this prayer for your family:

Father, I thank You that Your mercy and goodness are following my family all the days of their life and that they will dwell in Your house forever. And Father, I thank You that Your grace covers them everywhere they go.

Chapter 3

CHOICES, ALERTNESS, AND SECURITY

BEANIE WEENIE RELIGION

When you are preparing a meal, you have to make choices. For instance, if you plan a meal of beanie weenies, you can save by cutting up several hot dogs and adding them to the beans, or you can use a whole package and give your family a larger portion of meat.

The same applies in your walk with the Lord. You can come to church when you feel like it, give offering when you choose, pray when you think about it, and have a beanie weenie relationship with the Lord; or you can make God top priority and have a life *whole* and *complete* in Him.

Get to know Him personally and to know His great loving heart. He loves you and is willing to give you His best. You too can know Him and then give Him your best!

> Shout with joy before the Lord, O earth! Obey him gladly; come before him, singing with joy. Go through his open gates with great thanksgiving; enter his courts with praise. Give thanks to him and bless his name.
> —Psalm 100:1–2, 4

LANDMARKS

When you move into a new area, you have to learn the landmarks around you to locate your street and directions to your home. We lived in an area once where there were two ways to get to our home. One street had a dead tree with an osprey's nest in it. One day when a storm came through, the tree was blown down and the landmark was destroyed. The other street had a blue sign. Even if you couldn't read the street sign at night, you could look for the blue sign and know where to turn. One day the blue sign was taken down; that landmark was also destroyed, but by then I had learned where to turn without the landmarks.

The same applies to your Christian walk. When you become a Christian, you start looking to others for your security, but there comes a time when the people you look up to and depend on move, and things change. The tree you built your nest in may be cut down, or the signs you were using for direction disappear.

However, if you have learned to keep your eyes and focus on Jesus, you will have a strong sense of direction, and you can grow and develop in your Christian walk and know that your security is not in things or others, but it is in Him.

> What is faith? It is the confident assurance that something we want is going to happen. It is the certainty that what we hope for is waiting for us, even though we cannot see it up ahead.
> —Hebrews 11:1

WISDOM

Many years ago, two guys took a small jon boat and went over to an island at night to kill alligators for their hides. They wore headlights and would ride around and use a pole to push the boat around the water, which wasn't very deep. They used the headlight to shine the gator eyes, which would glow red when a light was turned on them.

When they did spot a gator, they would shoot him. They shot one gator and stunned him instead of killing him. They thought he was dead, so they dragged him into the boat with them. He was about a ten-foot gator.

They continued on poling around the lake looking for another one. While doing so, the gator, which was in the bottom of the boat between their legs, came to and started thrashing around. One of them grabbed an ax and tried to hit the gator. He missed the gator and chopped a hole in the bottom of the boat. The boat sank, they lost their gator, and then had to wade through the gator-infested pond back to shore. Their evening was ruined. They saw gator eyes glowing red all around them, and they were glad to arrive back to shore.

When you are in a dark place and it seems the enemy is all around, let the truth and the light of Jesus shine on the situation, and watch God bring you to a place of safety.

BE ALERT

My son and his family used to live by a river that flowed into a canal behind their house. While we were having dinner one day, we looked out to see a large, dead fish that had gotten stuck on some tree roots in the water.

As we watched, an alligator came along and very slowly stalked the fish. He did not move on his prey until he had watched a while. Then all of a sudden, he pounced and started eating the dead fish.

This is the way the Enemy, Satan, does. He watches and listens to see where you are spiritually. He cannot read your mind, but he can hear what you speak and see your actions. Then he can pounce on you and plant unhealthy thoughts into your mind.

You do not have to be dead spiritually for him to attack, but your behavior makes you vulnerable. You need to guard your life, keep the hedge of protection around you, have your mind and heart filled with the life and thoughts of Jesus, and walk in the power of the Holy Spirit.

Don't get stuck in the roots of despair, trials, and problems of the day. Stay alert and filled with life in the Holy Spirit so that you will be aware and recognize the Enemy when he comes around.

God is calling your heart to His heart and drawing you into a deeper walk with Him. As you read your Bible, pray, meditate on Him, and let His love flow through you and draw you into His holy presence and into a deep, heart-to-heart experience with Him.

Chapter 4

BRUISES, COURAGE, AND MOTIVATION

EATING AN APPLE

THERE ARE TIMES WHEN EATING AN APPLE THAT THERE will be brown spots on it. Bruising may cause the spots, or if you keep looking you will occasionally discover a worm in the apple, which is the cause of the bad spots.

If you leave the worm in and it gets to the core, the apple will be destroyed. If you take the worm out in time, the apple can be saved.

When a person's emotions get bruised, whether by a situation they caused, something someone else did, or some incident that happened, they get disgruntled, and you hear them complaining and grumbling. It may be about their job, church, home, or their personal life, and they come to you to vent their negativity.

Instead of letting them cause you to lose your peace and get you off course for your life, stay removed from the situation but listen to them long enough to discover the reason for the bruised spot, or worm. Then you can help them deal with the bruise or pluck out the worm, and the person's emotions can be healed.

> We can rejoice, too, when we run into problems and trials for we know that they are good for us—they help

us learn to be patient. And patience develops strength of character in us and helps us trust God more each time we use it until finally our hope and faith are strong and steady.

—Romans 5:3–4

BE STRONG! BE COURAGEOUS!

One day I was walking down a sidewalk on my way home. A tiny dog was outside, and when he saw me coming, he started running, half-looking back and whining, scared.

As soon as his master stepped out so that he could see him, this little dog turned around and started running at me, barking with confidence. It was so funny to see his transformation when he knew he had backup.

Sometimes you feel like the hardships of life are chasing you, and you feel very scared and insecure. But, when you go to the Lord in prayer, you realize that right there in front of you and your circumstance is a big God looking after you. All of a sudden when you realize this, you can then run toward your problems in power and with confidence.

> "Be Strong! Be Courageous! Do not be afraid of them! For the Lord your God will be with you. He will neither fail you nor forsake you."
>
> —Deuteronomy 31:6

BITTER OR BETTER

When things surround you and trouble comes, you may just plain feel you are the only one in the whole wide world doing anything for God. Your motivation for doing the deeds you have undertaken may be wrong. You take your eyes off Jesus. You could begin to let bitter feelings start creeping into your heart.

The solution to the problem is this:

1. Get your eyes back on Jesus.

2. Look around you; there are a lot of things going on that someone other than you had to put forth a lot of effort to accomplish.

3. Do not take on more than you can handle; learn when to say yes and when to say no.

4. Check your motivation; make sure everything you do is because of your total, committed love for God and His kingdom, nothing else.

When you go through this checklist and your heart is pure in all you do, then you will have praise in your heart, all your bitterness will leave, and the more you praise God, the better you will feel.

You will not be *bitter*, but you will be *better*!

> I will praise you, my God and King, and bless your name each day and forever. Great is Jehovah! Greatly praise him! His greatness is beyond discovery!
>
> —Psalm 145:1–3

Chapter 5

TEMPTATION, PRAYER, AND GOOD THINGS

TROUBLE

ONE TIME WHEN OUR CHILDREN WERE YOUNG, WE HAD A dog named "Trouble." When he was a puppy, he lived up to his name with his antics, such as turning on the hot water heater spigot while we were gone.

One day when my son was fishing in a canal near our house, Trouble went with him. My son started tempting fate by dangling the fishing lure in front of the dog's nose—playing with *trouble*. Our dog Trouble grabbed the lure, and the hook stuck in his mouth. Soon, with the hook and dog on one end and the fishing pole in my son's hand on the other end, the dog and my son went running down the road to the house seeking help, both yelling at the top of their lungs. You can imagine the commotion it caused. The dog was rescued and everything turned out OK.

If you play with sin or temptation, it may look like fun and a good thing. But, when the devil gets his hook in you, it isn't fun anymore. It can cause you much despair. You and trouble may go running down the road towards a loving and caring God yelling, "God, help! God, help!"

Don't forget—it hurts worse to pull the hook out than it did when the hook went in. So it's best not to play with trouble.

PATIENCE

My husband loves to fish. He wanted me to go with him sometimes, but I didn't have the patience. One morning, he came home after working the late-night shift. He decided he would like to go fishing before he went to sleep. He asked me to go with him, but I didn't want to go. So he said, "If you will go, I will cast one time. If I don't catch anything, we will come home." The salt-water canal where we fished wasn't too far from the house, so I said OK.

We went. He took his rod and reel out of the car and got ready for his prize. He watched the water and cast out his line. Along came a large fish, and with the first cast he caught a twenty-nine and three-quarter pound snook. Then he put the fish, the pole, and me in the car and took us home. He was rewarded for his patience.

Don't give up! Pray without ceasing for your family. It may seem nothing is happening, but if you don't give up, the Holy Spirit will draw them. And one day, you *will* get your prize!

WAIT ON THE LORD

> But they that wait upon the LORD shall renew their strength; they shall mount up with wings like eagles; they shall run and not be weary; and they shall walk, and not faint.
>
> —Isaiah 40:31, KJV

Many times, things in your life may seem to be unstable. You say, "God, what is going on?" You need to look beyond the immediate circumstances. God allows situations to arise in your life to bring things to the surface, such as pride, rebellion, anger, selfishness, anything that may be hindering your relationship with the Lord. You may not know that you are harboring hidden things in your heart until situations arise and these feelings are exposed to you.

God allows things to occur to bring these emotions to the surface so that you will realize they are there and, with the help of the Holy Spirit, deal with them. Then submit your will to His will to perfect you. You cannot be defeated as long as you are obedient, yielded, and submitted totally to God's perfect will for your life. Do not dwell on negative thoughts, because they are tools of the enemy to steal your joy. Let God perfect you for His purpose in your life.

Seek the Lord, wait upon Him, and submit to His will for your life.

> They that wait upon the Lord shall renew their strength; they shall mount up with wings like eagles; they shall run, and not be weary; and they shall walk and not faint.
>
> —Isaiah 40:31, KJV

Every Good Thing

> But then I will come and do for you all the good things I have promised, and bring you home again. For I know the plans I have for you, says the Lord. They are plans for good and not for evil, to give you a future and a hope.
>
> —Jeremiah 29:10–11

As you have gone through life growing and developing in your relationship with the Lord, there may have been times when you had to deal with problems that came into your path, such as hurt and pain caused from misunderstandings, emotional insecurities, depression, or fear that perhaps resulted from illness or financial difficulties. You may have gone through upsetting situations that helped you to understand what was happening in some areas of your life. As you prayed and sought God for revelation, He gave you peace and understanding that helped to bring maturity in your spiritual walk.

During these times, there may be other voices speaking to you, telling you of promises that may or may not be for you. Don't lasso and pull in wrong promises or hope. Keep your eyes and ears tuned into what the Holy Spirit is saying to you so that you will not be led astray and miss God's promises. Healing may be an ongoing process, and you may still be dealing with some areas, but you must have peace and trust God, knowing that He loves you and His plans for you are good plans "to give you a future and a hope."

As you develop, the Holy Spirit will continually reveal to you some area that needs purging in order for you to go higher and higher in your relationship with the Lord. But there comes a time when a particular season in your life brings you to a place where it seems to be the hardest task you have ever undertaken. It seems like just before your breakthrough, you are hit with the hardest battle.

As you go through these battles, you should recognize the challenges set before you are for that time and season of your life. Even though it may be an ongoing healing process, you can have peace and the assurance that God is in control, and in Him, all is well. Then seek Him about the promises that He spoke to you in your spirit for that season. He is always with you in and through every situation; but during these times, as you are seeking Him in prayer and reading the Bible, you will be comforted by the promises you receive from Him. Even though it is hard at times, the Holy Spirit of God is with you, comforting you all the way through, guiding you, and bringing you safely to the other side of your situation. Troubles may come and go, but God's Word never fails.

> But Abraham never doubted. He believed God, for his faith and trust grew ever stronger, and he praised God for this blessing even before it happened.
>
> —Romans 4:20

Chapter 6

PRAISE, STRENGTH, AND PROVISION

Looking Good

SEVERAL YEARS AGO, WE HAD A CAR THAT WAS VERY PRETTY on the outside, but after driving it for a while, we started having problems with the engine. We had to take it to the garage several times for repair. It still looked good on the outside, but on the inside it had several needs that had to be taken care of.

At times in your life, situations may come your way that cause great distress to you on the inside. If your distress continues and you don't deal with the cause, it can also begin to take its toll on you, even in your outer appearance. Most of the time no matter how you hurt on the inside, you keep a great outward appearance. You will keep your hair looking good, wear nice clean clothes, and wear a beautiful smile. The only way another person could tell that you are in trouble is—if they look close enough—they can see the pain in your eyes. So many times though, others are so involved with their own circumstances that they don't look close enough to see your pain.

With an automobile, when trouble comes, you have to go to someone that can repair the problem. In life, you have to do the same. If the condition is physical, you may have to go to a doctor. If it is emotional, you may have to go see a counselor. If it is financial, you may need help from a financial advisor. But in all things, you need to go to Jesus. He is the only ultimate cure for any problem. If you need a job, He is your way-maker; if you are in financial distress, He is your provider. If you are in an emotional dilemma, He is your peace. Whatever your crisis might be, you can depend on Him. You have to do your part and, if needed, seek help, but Jesus will be with you in any circumstance. He wraps His love around all your concerns!

A few years ago, my husband's job took him to another city away from where we lived, so we relocated. In his daily work activities, he met a man with a wife and child. The man had been very ill and was still not well. Due to his health, he hadn't been able to work. Since we had recently moved to the area, I needed a job. My husband had previously met a businessman that was looking for an office person, and after talking with my husband, he planned to give the job to me. When my husband found out about the condition of the man with the family, he went to this businessman and asked him if he could give the man a job. He said, "If I give him a job, it will have to be your wife's job." So we talked and decided the right thing to do was to give the other person the job, so he hired him. Later, the businessman went to church, and after service told an attorney that went to the same church what had transpired. The attorney got in touch with my husband and said, "Tell your wife to come and see me." I went, and after interviewing me, he hired me. There was a triple-fold blessing in this: (1) A family in great need was blessed with a job. (2) I didn't have to go looking for a job; the job came to me. (3) The business was blessed, because God gave me the skills to do a good job for them.

When you get the personal engine of your life running smoothly, then you can look and feel good on the inside and on the outside. Your eyes and countenance will be bright and shiny, showing a happy, healthy person.

> "Don't hide your light! Let it shine for all; let your good deeds glow for all to see, so that they will praise your heavenly Father."
>
> —Matthew 5:15–16

TEMPLE OF THE LORD

> Solomon now decided that the time had come to build a temple for the Lord and a palace for himself. "It is going to be a wonderful temple because he is a great God, greater than any other."
>
> —2 Chronicles 2:1, 5

Your body is the temple of the Lord. You are in the process of building a house for the Lord. His house will be a strong house, filled with praise and worship, and founded on God's Word.

Solomon built his house with the best timbers, gold, silver, iron, stone, and fine linens. You can build your house with the best, too, as you lift your praises unto God, worship from your heart, and study God's Word. As you do these things, your house will be built with a good, solid foundation—one that will be great, for great is our God above all gods. (See Psalm 135:5.) But it must begin in your heart. You must have a pure, loving heart towards the Father, one that says, "Father, not my will, but Your will be done." (See Luke 22:42.)

WIN THE RACE

A great racehorse has beauty, potential, strength, and speed—all the qualities to be a winner. However, he cannot win a race and use his great assets and potential just standing around the pasture feeding. He has to get on the track and, with the help of his trainer, develop and use his great strengths to become a winner!

As Christians, many times we have a desire to be used by God in service for His kingdom. We pray, "Lord, use me." With the power of the Holy Spirit, we have great potential to do mighty exploits for God. But to develop our potential and assets, we have to apply ourselves by being committed to God's house, praying, reading the Bible, and being faithful to His conditions.

Then we have to get on the racetrack (get involved), run the race, and be a winner!

> In a race, everyone runs but only one person gets first prize. So run your race to win. To win the contest you must deny yourselves many things that would keep you from doing your best. An athlete goes to all this trouble just to win a blue ribbon or a silver cup, but we do it for a heavenly reward that never disappears.
>
> —1 Corinthians 9:24–25

LIVING IN THE LIGHT

I went into a dark room one day, and my husband, who was standing nearby, teased me saying, "It will cost you a quarter to come in." I proceeded to walk in. Then he said, "It will cost you fifty cents to turn the light on." I said, "That's OK, I'll stay in the dark; it's free."

I started thinking about that and realized that is the way we live our life at times. We are not willing to pay the price to be in the light. We choose to stay in the dark, thinking it is free. But it isn't free.

There is a high price to pay if you stay ignorant and in the dark about things. The enemy of your soul lives in the dark places. He will lead you around and ultimately destroy you, unless you let the light of Jesus shine into your dark places and expose the enemy. Then you will be free and live in victory—a victorious life!

> For every child of God can obey him, defeating sin and evil pleasure by trusting Christ to help him.
>
> —1 John 5:4

Father, I put my full confidence and trust in you, to bring healing and strength in every part of me, and I know that I can overcome through the blood of Jesus.

Chapter 7

FAITHFULNESS, TRUST, ENDURANCE, AND INTERVENTION

Don't Interfere

I was raised in a Christian home and gave my heart to Jesus at an early age. I would never dream of doing anything that was not pleasing to the Lord or knowingly interfere with anyone else in his or her Christian walk and service unto the Lord.

My husband served in law enforcement for several years. Our children were young, so I was at home with them. My husband, when possible, would come home for lunch.

One day, I had prepared lunch at the usual time. When he arrived, he had someone with him. I had not expected company, so I gave him my lunch. I knew I could eat later. The man with him was thin and dressed in old-looking clothes. He looked like perhaps he was homeless or, to use the common term back then, a tramp. Even though he looked like this, he seemed clean.

After lunch as they prepared to leave, I graciously said my good-byes. But, to my astonishment, he poked his long bony finger at me. I backed up until I hit my TV stereo console and couldn't go any farther. He said with his finger pointed at me, "Don't you ever do anything to interfere with your husband serving the Lord!" I indignantly replied, "I would never!" They left, but I have never forgotten the incident.

Since then I have had to remember and, through tears at times, submit to God's plan for our lives. If you feel He is asking something of you, before making a decision, you must discuss it thoroughly, pray, and, if needed, seek counsel. Even though it is hard to make changes or give up your stable life, if you are faithful and trust Him, God always gives back much more than He ever asks of you.

BATTEN DOWN THE HATCHES

When a ship goes out to sea and a storm comes, they close and latch all the hatches and portholes before they ride out the storm. This is called battening down the hatches.

We were going through some difficult times financially at one time, and we had been trusting God to see us through. I had done really well, but I got concerned one day. My husband was talking to me, showing me I needed to keep trusting. I was very sincere and told him, "I *am* trusting God!" He kept insisting, "No, you aren't. You need to trust God." I kept insisting, "I am trusting God." He said, "No, you aren't." I started crying, not over the circumstances, but because I didn't know what to do. So I said, "If I'm not, then I don't know how. I am trusting." He said, "OK."

I left the bedroom and went into the kitchen to the sink, where we had a serving window with a counter from the kitchen to the living area. He came out of the bedroom and stood on the other side of the counter, across from me. He looked me in the eye and said what God had told him, "You aren't trusting Him! You are battening down the hatches, and riding out the storm. All you did was grit your teeth and hold on until it was over. You thought you were trusting, but you weren't. If you had truly been trusting, you would have peace, and no concern." All of a sudden I got it. My husband said it was like a cork popping out of a bottle when I finally got the revelation of what he was saying.

If you are in a place where you really need to trust God about a situation, don't batten down the hatches in fear and ride out the storm. Trust God, and let Him give you peace.

MY BURDEN IS LIGHT

Many times people see others that have committed their life to God and are walking in top places and positions, and they want to be in a place like that. They seek the accolades and recognition of being up front.

When they get there, if they have not paid the price of commitment, they find only a lot of hard work, and they start complaining. They are not getting the recognition they thought would come in that place.

After all the miracles and ministry, when Jesus got to the top, He was crucified. But what happened later? He rose again, victorious. There is greater success after the sacrifice.

In order to get to the top and be a success in the Lord, you must give up your selfish desires, be willing to release the things that would hinder your relationship with the Lord, and seek only Jesus. Then when you get to the top and you find that there are no accolades but rather only hard work, you won't say, "Where is the recognition?" The honor comes when you lay down your own selfish desires and want only God's will for your life; then you walk in the glorious presence of the Holy Spirit. All the glory belongs to Jesus! It is a joy to touch lives and see them changed as you minister God's love to them.

> "Come to Me, all you who labor and are heavy laden, and I will give you rest. Take My yoke upon you, and

learn from Me, for I am gentle and lowly in heart, and you will find rest for your souls. For My yoke is easy and My burden is light."

—Matthew 11: 28–30, NKJV

WORDS

May my spoken words and unspoken thoughts be pleasing even to you, O Lord my Rock and my Redeemer.

—Psalm 19:14

This is a scripture that may have been familiar to you for many years. But have you really gotten a revelation on its meaning?

Many times when things are not going well and you are hit from all sides with problems and difficulties, you may start to complain and say, "Why is this happening? I don't understand what's going on," and so forth.

Read the scripture again:

"May my spoken words": Be careful what comes from your mouth.

"And my unspoken thoughts": Are your thoughts pure?

"Be pleasing even to you, O Lord": Is God pleased with your words, and attitudes?

"My Rock": He is your strength when you feel weak.

"My Redeemer": He is your Salvation, and He delivers you from your problems and situations.

RESPONSIBILITY

While I was sitting at my desk one day in a beautiful office complex, I had just printed a couple of forms and was stapling them together for our children's church. I looked around the complex at the offices around me and thought, "They must be doing much bigger things than I."

Then the thought came to my mind, "What I am doing may be much more important, because what I have here is molding and developing minds that will affect lives and souls for eternity!"

Another time, I observed an usher taking responsibility for the offering buckets. He would see that the buckets were available for every service. I thought, "How important this empty bucket is. When it is in its place, it provides the means of supplying the needs of God's kingdom!"

Sometimes the things you do may seem very insignificant. The things you do at your place of work or your job assignment at church may seem very small to you, but to God and His kingdom, every place must be filled.

Look beyond your empty bucket. God sees, and He alone knows what you do that affects His plans here on Earth and for eternity!

HE REALLY CAN, WILL, AND IS

He really can

Jesus is your waymaker! You can take what you have, lift it up to Jesus to be blessed, and He will miraculously multiply it and meet your need!

He really will

He is your security! When you are being tossed to and fro in your storms, Jesus will walk on the water with you, get in your boat, and lead you safely to the other side, to a place of peace and rest in Him.

He really is

He is your Savior! Because Jesus died on the cross and rose again, He opened up the way for you to walk with Him and have communion with Him. So *rejoice*, for the Lord has opened up the way for you, right now, to have life, and have it more abundantly. And He opened up the way for you to have eternal life to live forever and forever with Him, throughout all eternity.

Jesus really is all you will ever need. If you will believe and accept Him as your personal Lord and Savior and be obedient to what He asks of you in each season of your life, you can have a wonderful life here on earth with Him and have heaven to look forward to in your future. (See Mark 6:41–52; Luke 23:46; 24:6–7.)

The Cat's Meow

I was visiting my son and his family. They had a cat that had been like a family member for years, as well as a little black-and-white stray kitten named Boots that their daughter, a cat lover, had recently found and brought home.

My son and his family had gone to work and school, so I was alone at home. I was sitting on the couch in their living room, Boots was outside playing, and their family cat was on the arm of the couch that I was sitting on. They had two couches in their living room. The cat and I were on one; the other couch was by the front door. Boots decided she wanted to come in, so she went to the screen door and climbed up the screen. I told her to get down. She didn't, so I went over and shook the door and firmly said no, hoping she would get down. She didn't listen to me. The whole time, the family cat was watching me very intently. All of a sudden, the family cat made a leap from the arm of one couch across the room, touching the floor one time, then onto the arm of the other couch. She hissed and gave that little kitten a good scolding. I was so surprised. It was like she knew the kitten wasn't listening to me, so she would take care of the situation. It was priceless!

You may get into situations at times when problems seem to be climbing your screen door of life and harassing you. You try to handle the situation to no avail. Then God steps in and intervenes in behalf of your problem or situation, and says, "Back off! Enough!" God loves you and wants you to look to Him for comfort and help. You do all you can, but when that isn't enough, you have a loving, heavenly Father that is always watching and intervening on your behalf.

Chapter 8

CHARACTER, WISDOM, AND GOD'S ARMOR

CONFIDENTIALITY

I ONCE HAD INFORMATION AND WAS IN A POSITION, DUE TO my knowledge of the situation and my character, that I felt I should honor the confidentiality of the information. Later, I was standing near other people having a conversation, when one of them began spilling out what they seemed to know about the incident. I was annoyed that I had to remain silent, as this person was getting the ears of those around. But I remained silent.

At home that evening, I sat down to read my Bible and it opened to Proverbs 18:7 (NKJV), so I read it. "A fool's mouth is his destruction, And his lips are the snare of his soul." Boy, that went deep into my spirit, and I haven't forgotten it.

You may not need to be too concerned about what others do, but try to keep your own heart, mind, and spirit pure and clean before your heavenly Father, God. Do your best to be pleasing to Him.

BUILDING YOUR HOUSE

When you build a house, the first thing you do is contact a master contractor and build the foundation. You install the plumbing pipes, pour the cement slab, put up foundation walls, install the wiring, and put on the roof. These steps to building a house are not pretty, but they are permanent and necessary.

After all the foundation is complete, you start adding the fluff, or beauty. You paint, install the carpet or nice flooring, put up curtains, and select beautiful furniture. If you decide this isn't what you want, you can change colors, curtains, or furniture, but the foundation is still there, solid and unmoved.

You may feel sometimes that things are shaky and upsetting in your life. You feel at times that you work so hard and others always seem to get the credit, or that perhaps because their contribution is in the beauty area, they seem to get the thanks and recognition. Your talents may be in building the foundation, but remember, the other person worked hard, too. Their talents are in a different area than yours, but both are needed to complete the job.

When you feel hurt over a situation, you must call on the Master Contractor, Jesus, and get the foundation of your life solid in Him so that your house can withstand the rain and storms, the disappointment, hurt, or uncertain times. Get your heart set on preparing a solid, secure foundation for your life. The fluff or beauty will come after the foundation is complete. God sees your faithfulness, and if you trust Him, He will give you His joy and peace. You will be content, knowing that you are pleasing to Him and that, in His timing, He will reward you for all that you do.

Matthew 7:24–25 says:

> "All who listen to my instructions and follow them are wise, like a man who builds his house on solid rock. Though the rain comes in torrents, and the floods rise and the storm winds beat against his house, it won't collapse, for it is built on rock."

BOUNDARIES

When I lived on the east coast of Florida near the Atlantic Ocean, I marveled at the way the water would come in and go out, come in and go out, endlessly. Several times a storm would go by out at sea, or a northeaster would blow in, causing humongous waves. The waves would be high and the water would be higher up on shore, but no matter how large or small the waves, unless due to an extreme act of nature, they did not go farther than their set boundaries.

Seeing this, it makes the heart say, "How truly marvelous are your works, oh God. You truly are the Almighty, our powerful Creator, and Lord of all!"

Oh, the awesome, majestic power of God. Yet, He loves you so very much that He gave His only Son, Jesus—who left His home in heaven to come to earth and die so that you might be forgiven your sins, be restored back to the Father, and have eternal life with Him forever and ever.

> "Who decreed the boundaries of the seas when they gushed from the depths? Who clothed them with clouds and thick darkness, and barred them by limiting their shores, and said, 'Thus far and no farther shall you come, and here shall your proud waves stop!'"
>
> —Job 38:8–11

LET YOUR LIGHT SHINE

A few years back, I was very privileged to have the opportunity to make a trip to Israel. I saw so many wonderful things. Among the many sights, I saw the place where Jesus was born and walked, the Dead Sea, the Sea of Galilee, and the Mediterranean Sea. We went with a tour group and stayed busy from early morning to after dark.

On one of our trips one day, I looked up and saw a city on a high hill. I thought about the verse in the Bible, "You are the light of the world. A city that is set on a hill cannot be hidden" (Matt. 5:14, nkjv). Seeing this, I could see what Jesus was talking about.

It is so important that you live each day of your Christian walk knowing that people are watching you. You will either be sour, disgruntled, and show forth darkness; or, if your relationship is right with the Lord, you are praying, in the Word, and have God's Holy Spirit flowing through you, your life will shine with the light of God's love. Then you will be a blessing and touch the lives of people you come in contact with each day.

> "You are the light of the world. A city that is set on a hill cannot be hidden."
>
> —Matthew 5:14, nkjv

The Real Thing Versus Imitation

When my children were young, to economize, I decided to try mixing half powdered milk and half whole milk.

My sister-in-law was over one day with her three-year-old. I shared this with her, and she said, "If he will drink it, then it will be OK. He is very expressive about everything."

We poured a glass and watched his response. He tasted it and said, "Yuck!"

So it is with your walk with the Lord. Why mix imitation with the awesome glory of God that is yours for the taking? Do not exchange the real for imitation. Don't straddle the fence with apathy or indecision. Don't settle for the "yuck."

Go for the most powerful experience you could ever experience in your entire life; jump on in!

No wonder we are happy in the Lord! For we are trusting him. We trust his holy name. Yes, Lord, let your constant love surround us, for our hopes are in you alone.

—Psalm 33:21–22

ARMOR OF GOD

One day my little granddaughter wanted to go outside but didn't have her shoes on. She ran up to her mother and said, "Mommy, I have my feet on. Mommy, Mommy, I have my feet on!"

Do you have your feet on, or are your feet shod with the preparation of the gospel of peace?

Ephesians 6:11 (NKJV) says, "Put on the whole armor of God."

Father, you are my banner of protection over me. I cover myself with the blood of Jesus, and I pray a hedge of protection around my family and myself. I tear down the strongholds Satan has formed against me, and I refuse to receive any lies or deception of the enemy. I surrender myself totally and completely to you, Holy Spirit.

I put on the whole armor of God. My loins are girded about with truth, I have on the breastplate of righteousness, and my feet are shod with the preparation of the gospel of peace. I take up the shield of faith, so that I can quench all the fiery darts of the wicked. I put on the helmet of salvation, and I take up the sword of the Spirit, which is the word of God. (See Ephesians 6:11–17, NKJV.)

Trust God every day as you go about your daily activities of life. He is your strength and help in your time of need.

SURPRISE!

My husband and his friend would take his dad's truck and go to a sand dune on the bluff near their home. They would cut donuts in the field, get a running start, and then go up the hill real fast and jump the sand dune.

One day, without first checking the hill, they cut donuts in the field and got up speed to jump. When they got on top of the hill and were airborne, they realized someone had taken the dirt from the backside since the last time they went. They had a rough landing!

If it seems your road is always rocky and your landing always rough, maybe you should do a checklist on your pattern for running your life.

Are you looking around and removing the rocky things that you need to change—bad habits, hazardous situations that you could deal with, using caution when making a decision? Are you cutting donuts in your life and playing games instead of getting serious about your relationship with the Lord? Are you in the Word, praying, and asking God for direction before you run up the hill of life, or do you find you are airborne without checking the situation on the other side of your decision?

God loves you so much. He cares about you and wants to be in every part of your life. Receive Jesus as Lord and Savior of your life. Seek God, and let His Holy Spirit direct you in your decisions. Then even if your road is still rocky at times, you will have peace, knowing that you are not playing games, but have looked your situation in the face, dealt with it, and are trusting God to see you to the other side.

Chapter 9

VALUE, DIRECTION, AND PROTECTION

PEARL

When my granddaughter was eleven years old, her family moved from the town they had lived for a few years. When she went to the new school, several of the girls picked on her. They gave her a hard time about her clothes and called her names like "Fatty" and "Nerd," among others. This was devastating to her, as she was a pretty little girl and not any of these things.

One day she went to church, and they talked to them about school and how kids will pick on you. This really ministered to her. She related the experience to her mother with tears in her eyes. The very next day, things at school changed. She said, "Every kid at school was nice to me." And they were nice the rest of the year.

No matter where you come from or what circumstances you are in, God is forming you into a beautiful person.

As oysters lie in their oyster bed on the bank of a river or bay, as the water goes by and the sand and mud surround them; my husband shared that "the oyster opens up and as the water flows through, the oyster filters it. Sometimes a grain of sand flows through and causes an irritant. So when this happens, the oyster, in order to protect itself, forms a crust around the grain of sand, and sometimes a pearl is formed."

As an oyster deals with its irritant, you may do a similar thing to keep your irritants confined. Sometimes you put a shell around your emotions, but as you open up your heart and allow Jesus to heal your hurts, then you can be transformed like a beautiful pearl.

PEARL OF GREAT PRICE

I was shelling at the beach on the Atlantic Ocean one day, and I saw this beautiful colored shell. I reached down to pick it up, and my husband said, "That's just an oyster shell." I stood admiring it because the inside of the shell was so shiny and smooth and had such beautiful colors. Its colors caught my eye. I don't know if a pearl had ever been formed in it or not, but I do know its beauty caused me to stoop down and pick it up.

As you allow God to form you through good times and hard times, people will be attracted to your beautiful color, and they will stop by your life. Some may look and walk on by, but others will be attracted and stop by for a moment, and you will touch their life. Remember, it's the beauty and shine of the Lord that attracts them.

I still remember the beautiful oyster shell. Other pretty little shells passed it on their tumble through the waves and made it to shore. Someone picked them up, saw their beauty, and lovingly took them home with them. The little oyster shell kept faithfully tumbling and rolling on its way to far off places with no one giving much notice, until after years of being broken and polished by sand and waves, it washed up on shore.

Then one day, someone picks it up, and in amazement says, "It's an oyster shell! Look at all the beautiful colors." They may not want to take it home and may toss it back into the ocean. Still, because of its refinement from storms tossing it around, it not only possibly birthed and developed a pearl inside, but now it is beautiful to the one who takes time to stop and take a good look at the beauty it developed over time.

As an irritant in an oyster can form a pearl, the irritants in your life will be forming you into a beautiful pearl. A great price had to be paid in order to purify and form you as you walk through your lazy rolling waves, with the rough waves spraying in the wind. Your beauty will be not only internal but will also be seen on the outside.

> Again, the Kingdom of Heaven is like a pearl merchant on the lookout for choice pearls. He discovered a real bargain—a pearl of great value—and sold everything he owned to purchase it!
>
> —Matthew 13: 45–46

THE LIGHTHOUSE

My husband grew up in a town near the Atlantic Ocean. The bluff where he lived was on a river that flowed into a sound or bay, a body of water that went into the ocean.

Back when this country was first being settled, the big, tall ships that sailed from Europe would come over here empty. An empty boat isn't very sea-worthy, so before the ships left port in England, they would load the ships up with big rocks to keep it riding in the water like it should. Then when they would get to America, they would pull up along the coast somewhere and would dump the rocks—always in the same place.

On the Georgia coast, each area where they dumped the rocks formed three different sets of islands, nine altogether with three in each group. These islands are still there to this day. They are called ballast piles. Each set of three islands had a well drilled on them called an artesian well. An artesian well is a fresh water source that has enough natural water pressure that it doesn't need a pump to flow. How they did that so many years ago is really fascinating. Over the years, trees and vegetation grew on the ballast piles. You could climb up on the rocks, make your way through the trees and vegetation, and find the wells.

At night the stars and moon give light. It is dark, but you can still see from the light in the sky. But on a stormy night, it could be pitch black, making it hard to find your way around one of these islands. You could go the wrong way, which would take you out into the open water of the ocean instead of back the way you came, towards the river and home.

My husband had a very dear older gentleman friend that, due to an accident, had lost his sight. When he was around thirteen or fourteen years old, he and his friend were out in a boat one stormy night on the sound. My husband was steering the boat. Growing up in this area, he was very familiar with the river and sound, but because of the storm, it was so dark that he lost his bearings and didn't know which way to go. His friend said, "Can you see the light flashing from the lighthouse?" He looked around, and off in the distance, he could see streaks of light flashing in the night sky. They were out in the open water, and in order to get home he needed to find the ballast piles that were at the mouth of the river. If he went the wrong way, they could have gone to the ocean or run against sharp, dangerous obstacles. He had to know his way so that he could run a safe course.

As he watched the lighthouse light flashing in the night sky, at first it appeared only as streaks of light across the dark sky in the distance; then he could see in the sky the light shining through the atmosphere. When you get closer, as the light flashes, you can see silhouettes of the islands that you are looking for. His friend said, "Keep watching the flashes, and when the light comes around, follow the light down to the base where the light source originates. Then when you can tell where it comes from, steer directly towards the lighthouse." He followed his instructions and soon saw the dark shadows of the ballast piles. He then knew exactly where he was and how to get to the river and home.

If you have had a night storm and you have lost your way or have allowed obstacles that might sink you to get in your way, look for the light of God's direction and trust Him to lead you safely to a familiar place. Then you can find your way back home to a place of love and safety. His light will always lead you into His safe harbor.

> May the Lord bring you into an ever deeper understanding of the love of God and of the patience that comes from Christ.
>
> —2 Thessalonians 3:5

Do Not Be Afraid

Years ago, we were traveling down the road, pulling a tandem four-wheel trailer full of furniture. The loaded trailer was heavier than the car. The tire on the trailer went off the pavement and caused a flat tire. When this happened, the trailer started swinging back and forth until my husband lost control. He was fighting to correct it, but couldn't. The trailer was trying to pass the car.

My husband had to give driving his complete attention. Seeing the situation, I knew we were in deep trouble. It happened so quickly that all I could say was, "God, no! God, no!" In an instant, the trailer stopped swinging and was going straight down the road behind the car where it belonged. God delivered my family from a very bad place.

The children of Israel wandered in the wilderness for forty years and went through many difficulties. Sometimes in your life when things get tough and you find yourself in a wilderness of despair, discouragement, or disappointment that causes you to lose hope, just as God delivered the children of Israel, you too can be delivered. Trust Him!

Do not believe that the wilderness you are in will last forever. God hears your prayers and He can change your situation.

> And Moses said to the people, "Do not be afraid. Stand still, and see the salvation of the LORD, which He will accomplish for you today. For the Egyptians whom you see today, you shall see again no more forever. The LORD will fight for you, and you shall hold your peace."
>
> —Exodus 14: 13–14, NKJV

REAL OR BLUFF

Our family wanted a dog, and my husband loved German shepherds. We decided to go out and look at a litter of puppies. We always thought that if you picked out a dog with big feet, he would be a big dog one day. So we picked out a cute, adorable black-and-tan puppy with big feet. We brought him home and named him Flash. The kids had a ball playing with him.

Living in the country, we were always careful of strangers coming to our door. One day my husband was gone, and a couple of men stopped by. They said their vehicle had broken down, and they needed to use the telephone. I said, "I can't let you come in. I have a German shepherd. Give me the number you need to call, and I will call for you." About that time, one of the kids came through the door, and my little German shepherd puppy went galloping outside. We looked at each other and laughed. I tried a bluff, and it didn't work; I got exposed.

This is the way it is with the devil. He goes around bluffing you all the time. I know there are times when everything in your life goes sour, but sometimes it is just because the enemy is harassing you. Take a look at your situation and see if it is real or a bluff. Say, "No! No! In the name of Jesus, I recognize what is happening to me." Don't come against people, and you do not need to dwell on the devil. You need to recognize the situation, do what you need to do to correct your part, take control of your thoughts, draw close to Jesus, and let Him help to bring about the best solution for everyone concerned.

Guard your mouth and your behavior; don't say things that would bring about problems. Sometimes just saying or doing something at the right moment will change the attitude of the whole situation. Also remember, if another person is involved, God loves the person you are dealing with. Even if it is hard to see any good in him or her at the time, truth always prevails, and peace, restoration, and good times do come again.

FLASH

When our children were young, our German shepherd dog, Flash, would find and kill snakes. He would grab them by the back of the head, away from their fangs, and shake them until the head and tail separated.

We were in the process, with help, of building our own house. One day we went to town to buy a ready-framed door. We purchased the door and secured it in the trunk of our car. When we arrived home, my husband took the door out of the trunk and took it around to the back of the house. The children and I went into the house.

Our dog had a particular bark when he saw a snake—one bark for poisonous snakes and a different bark for non-poisonous snakes. Shortly after we got home, Flash started his poisonous snake bark. My oldest son, hearing the bark, went running out the front door to investigate. Not knowing whether the snake was under the porch or in the hedges that were along the front of the house on either side of the porch, he planned to jump far enough to get away from the danger. He took a running jump off the porch. Flash, who was very protective of us and knew the danger, leapt up and intercepted my son in mid air, knocking him backwards onto the porch. Flash then lunged into the hedge and pulled the snake out. The snake was latched onto his bottom lip. My husband, when he heard the commotion, went around to the front of the house to see what was going on. Flash shook the snake off, and it landed at my husband's feet. It immediately coiled up ready to strike again. My husband didn't dare move. He told my son, "Bring me my gun. Bring me my gun." He shot the snake behind the head, but didn't completely sever it. Flash grabbed the snake and started whipping it back and forth. The head flew off and buried its fangs in the back of my husband's hand. He flung it off, and it landed on the ground by his feet. The mouth was still snapping, trying to bite again. He said, "Lord, you took care of Paul when the serpent bit him, now take care of me." By then my husband had come into the bedroom and was making a tourniquet with his belt. I saw that something was wrong, so I asked if he had been bitten. As soon as he said yes, I started thinking, "Now I have to rush him to the hospital." Instead, my husband, who was in law enforcement, called the sheriff's department. In a very short time they arrived and took him to the hospital. While on the way, they called me and said, "We have made arrangements for the veterinarian to pick up Flash. You can make arrangements for your children and come on to the hospital."

I arrived at the hospital, but before I could get out of the car and go in to see about my husband, the sheriff's deputy met me outside and said, "You have to go back home. The vet is there, but Flash went under the house and won't come out. You have to get him out from under the house so that he can be treated." I hurried back home, leaving my husband in the care of the doctors and nurses in the hospital. The deputy and my son, who had gone to the hospital with them, came back to the house to assist.

When I arrived home, the vet was there. My son coaxed and helped Flash out from under the house and into the hands of the vet, who immediately started treating him, and took him to the veterinarian hospital. We then returned to the hospital to see about my husband.

They didn't give him a test to see if he would have a reaction; instead they went ahead and gave him five ampoules of antivenin. He had a reaction to the antivenin, and they thought they were going to lose him. He told me later that he had an out of the body experience. The nurse assisting the doctor was his friend and acquaintance for a number of years. With her emergency room nursing and his police work, they had worked together when he would bring injured and wounded people in. He saw the nurse a couple of days later and asked her, "Why did you walk out on me when I needed you?" She said, "Because you were dying, and I didn't want to see it." She was shocked that he saw her leave. She said, "How did you know that?" He had been looking down from above, and saw himself and her leave the room. He didn't know anything else until the next morning. The doctor came in and said, "I can't find any reason to keep you. Everything checks out and is OK." They were astonished at his quick recovery. He had very little swelling and only spent a day and a night in the hospital. God truly did take care of him.

Both my husband and Flash received national attention through an Associated Press story, and he was sent newspaper clippings from several states.

SAFETY

The house we had in the country sat on some acreage, with a dirt road in front of our house. Our house was built back a little from the road. During the rainy season, the road would get underwater; so to get the road up high enough that water would not come over it, we hired a company to come and push the dirt up from the side of the road to the middle.

One of our sons, not thinking of danger, thought it was a good place to play. However, the dirt in the ditch that was made by the road grader made quicksand when it rained. Our son stepped into the ditch and could not get out. Fortunately, the water was not over his head, but his feet and legs were stuck tight.

My husband and I were in the house, and all of a sudden we heard Flash barking out by the road and running up to our house. He kept running between the ditch and the house until we realized that he must be trying to tell us something. We followed him and found our son stuck in the quicksand. He was stuck so hard that my husband had to dig him out; his shoes stayed there.

We are thankful for that dog and for God's protection over our son's life.

> Reverence for God gives a man deep strength; his children have a place of refuge and security.
> —Proverbs 14:26

God's Protection

When we lived in the country, my youngest son had an experience that proved to him how much God loves us and covers our lives with His protection.

He tells the story:

> Thinking back on childhood, my mind is taken to the event in my life that strongly molds my belief in a higher power. As a boy of no more than six years of age, we were living in a part of Florida that was at the edge of the Everglades. While out during my day doing the things that little boys do, I was heading into the house, proceeding to run up the front steps and into our home, when suddenly that all-too-familiar sound of a rattler came thundering in my ears out from under the steps. Almost as suddenly as the sound appeared, I was whisked off of those steps and onto the hood of my Dad's car, which was parked in front of the house. Of course, being the age that I was, it only dawned on me to scream at the top of my lungs, 'Snake! Snake! Snake!'

In response, to my great pleasure my dad appeared, bigger than life, along with our German shepherd dog, Flash. Within just a matter of minutes, there were no longer steps going up to our house—they had been removed by Superman, my dad—and the snake was no longer among the living.

It never quite dawned on me how spectacular those events were in shaping my Christianity, until I grew older. Others may choose to believe differently, but I know that day God's angels whisked me from those steps onto the hood of that old car.

～

Because you have made the LORD, who is my refuge, Even the Most High, your dwelling place, No evil shall befall you, Nor shall any plague come near your dwelling; For He shall give His angels charge over you, To keep you in all your ways. In their hands they shall bear you up, Lest you dash your foot against a stone. You shall tread upon the lion and the cobra, The young lion and the serpent you shall trample underfoot. "Because he has set his love upon Me, therefore I will deliver him; I will set him on high, because he has known My name. He shall call upon Me, and I will answer him; I will be with him in trouble; I will deliver him and honor him; With long life I will satisfy him, And show him My salvation."

—Psalm 91:9–16, NKJV

Chapter 10

OBEDIENCE, DISCOURAGEMENT, AND GOD'S PRESENCE

POWER

I HAVE SEEN CARS THAT WERE JUST BEAUTIFUL ON THE outside. The paint job was almost perfection and the interior looked new, but it either needed a lot of work or a new motor on the inside. If you feel you are spiritually run down and need a little repair or a new motor on the inside, remember:

1. Don't be anxious, but trust God in all things.

2. Jesus Christ is the same yesterday, today, and forever.

3. He will never fail you.

The Holy Spirit is the power that keeps you running! Pray this prayer:

Lord, my body needs a jump start! Fill me with the quickening of your Holy Spirit; so that whatever comes my way today, I will be alert and filled with energy to encourage others that walk through my life. Your presence will bring a smile to my face and joy in my spirit that will draw those who need a touch from You. I ask for the power of the Holy Spirit to rise up and flow through me with Your enabling power that brings forth victory in my life and the lives of those that You send my way. Make me Your vessel, filled to overflowing. As I pour out, You will keep filling me up with Your living water, flowing and running over, spilling out to those around me. Then those that need a jump start will find that fuel to get them started on their way to a life of fullness and fulfillment, in You.

"I will never, never fail you nor forsake you." ... Jesus Christ is the same yesterday, today, and forever.

—Hebrews 13:5; 8

YOU WILL REVIVE ME

Don't you yet understand? Don't you know by now that the everlasting God, the Creator of the farthest parts of the earth, never grows faint or weary? No one can fathom the depths of his understanding. He gives power to the tired and worn out, and strength to the weak. Even the youths shall be exhausted, and the young men will all give up. But they that wait upon the Lord shall renew their strength. They shall mount up with wings like eagles; they shall run and not be weary; they shall walk and not faint.

—Isaiah 40:28–31

I would like to encourage you to allow the Holy Spirit of God to revive you. Though you may walk in the midst of trouble, let God heal your broken heart. If you are dealing with death in the family, concerns about your children, unforgiveness, your marriage, job situations, or concerns about your future—whatever your situation is—God is with you, and He cares. Bring your troubles to Jesus. Talk to Him and tell Him your thoughts and feelings. Draw close to Him, and let His healing power cover, heal, and bring you to a place of peace in Him. Know that you are not alone, but your loving Father, God, is with you.

You have prayed until it seems you have done all you can; now know that your troubles are in God's hands. Having done all, trust Jesus to save and keep you. Then allow Him to bring His peace, forgiveness, and healing to you and the situations in your life. God loves you and is concerned about the things that affect you.

Praise the Lord as you haven't in the past. Let all those things of yesterday, today, and tomorrow slip away. Allow the Holy Spirit to renew your spirit, mind, and soul. Exalt God, and He will bless and lift you up.

Expect Miracles

When you have given your heart to Jesus and as you grow and develop in your walk with the Lord, you may have a desire to tell others of the wonderful life that can be theirs if they will surrender their life to Jesus and accept Him as their Lord and Savior. You may feel the love and compassion of the Lord to touch them with God's love, and, as He directs, to minister healing, joy, and blessings to their life.

As a Christian you have the right, in the name of Jesus, to go out and minister deliverance and healing and to witness and win souls to the kingdom of God. You can let them know that the living God is on their side, and through the authority and name of Jesus, you can help them face and deal with the strongholds that have tried to wreck their life and steal their health and joy.

You are serving an awesome God, who is going before you to prepare the way and is standing mightily with you as you bring forth the harvest for His kingdom! Expect miracles!

> Keep a close watch on all you do and think. Stay true to what is right and God will bless you and use you to help others.
>
> —1 Timothy 4:16

BE A WORSHIPER

A minister was going through his church after service one evening shaking hands and greeting the people. He came to me and greeted me. I said, "I really got blessed tonight!" Then he said to me, "You got a *look-on* blessing." He observed that I was blessed by and seeing others be blessed, though I was merely sitting and watching, not participating in the worship myself.

When you watch a Christian program on television or come to service and submit your heart and soul to worshiping and praising God, you receive the holy presence of God into your very being. Then as the Word from the man of God comes forth, a dynamic spiritual encounter happens. You will begin to hear and see in your spirit what God is doing and saying to you and to the church body.

Then as you receive and let His presence flow freely, you will have a dynamic power in you to go forth in your personal walk with God.

Don't be a *look-on* participant—be a *true* spiritual worshiper!

> I was glad when they said to me, "Let us go into the house of the LORD.
>
> —Psalm 122:1, NKJV

Little Foxes

The little foxes are ruining the vineyards. Catch them,
for the grapes are all in blossom.

—Song of Solomon 2:15

The "little foxes" this passage refers to include anything
that is stealing your peace and joy in the Lord. The harvest
is ripe, but if you let the foxes spoil your vineyard and steal
your fruit of the Spirit, you will not be equipped to reap
the harvest.

> "If you are willing and obedient, You shall eat the good
> of the land; But if you refuse and rebel, You shall be
> devoured by the sword"; For the mouth of the Lord
> has spoken.
>
> —Isaiah 1: 19–20, NKJV

Discouragement comes when you keep getting hit with
one problem after the other. Perhaps you have done all you
know to do, and it seems there is no end to it all. You have put
up fences and walls around your heart and life to keep from
being hurt, but the little foxes continue to find a way in.

Don't let discouragement be the enemy that brings you
down. Keep trusting. Do it Gods way!

> "And he shall say to them, 'Hear, O Israel: Today you
> are on the verge of battle with your enemies. Do not let
> your heart faint, do not be afraid, and do not tremble
> or be terrified because of them; for the Lord your God
> is He who goes with you, to fight for you against your
> enemies, to save you.'"
>
> —Deuteronomy 20:3–4, NKJV

Are you coming to the place in your life where you are on the verge of waging war against your problems? You have had enough. You have decided, "No more! I will not let my enemy of discouragement, fear, illness, drugs, alcohol, stress, or financial lack defeat me any longer. I am going to fight back and not let the enemy destroy me. I will not faint or be afraid. I will not tremble because of them. For the Lord my God is with me, to fight for me against my problems, and he will save me."

Pray this prayer:

> *Lord, I surrender my life totally to You today. Help me to remove the walls of defense that I have built around my heart and life. Help me to be strong and not vulnerable as I remove these walls. Heal and deliver me, and I will give you all the praise, honor, and the glory, in the name of Jesus. Amen!*

SUBMISSION

In my walk in the Lord, I always loved Him with all my heart and thought He was first in my life. If anyone had asked me about my salvation, I would have very firmly said, "Yes, Jesus is Lord of my life!"

My husband and I had been serving the Lord for many years doing what He called us to do in each season of our lives. After a period of years of service to the Lord, when our children were grown and married and we had no one but ourselves to be responsible for, God called my husband into a period of total commitment to Him through hours of prayer.

During this period of decision, he lost his job. No matter how many times he tried, he could not get a job. Finally, after much discussion with each other and earnest prayer, knowing we had heard God and that there was a purpose for his involvement in prayer ministry at the time, we submitted to the call to prayer on his life. I had a job and continued working so that we had an income, but I didn't make enough to handle all the monthly bills. I said, "If this is what God is requiring of us for you to be totally walking in faith and God's will, I am willing to do anything, even if it means losing the house."

It started looking like we would have to give up our home, and my husband would tell me, "I will give up and find a job." I said, "God gave me this house! No, you do what God called you to do."

Finally the time came that we would have to give the house up. Again, my husband had me make the decision. I said, "When I thought I could keep the house, I was willing to give it up. Now, I have to get real. Am I giving lip service, or do I mean with all my heart that I will do what it takes for the Lord?" So I told my husband, "We will give the house up." After that decision, God provided for us in so many ways. It was a joy to be taking a faith walk and watching God's miracles time and time again. It was very hard at times, and we really had to trust God.

During these times, you are being prepared for God's purpose for your life. We didn't know it at the time of our decision, but we later moved to another state and would have had to give up the house anyway. God knows your future. You go through preparation stages for a season, but you have to recognize when each season is over. After several years of service and preparation, we were sent out by our pastor and leadership to do God's plan for our life.

God does not require the same of everyone. You may have to give up something that will hinder God's plan for your life in your future. But if it doesn't affect your future, He may allow you to keep it. He wants your obedience and for you to put Him first in your life and be in tune to what the Holy Spirit is saying to you.

If you feel He is telling you to make changes that would seriously affect you and your family, you need to talk to each other, seek God diligently, and know you are without a doubt hearing Him. You also need to seek counsel with your pastor. Let him pray and seek God's counsel for you. If you go out before you are prepared, it could cause you to get discouraged and disillusioned. Don't go on your own. You need the counsel and blessing of your leadership in your decision. Whatever service and ministry areas in your church you are called to—cleaning the church or church grounds, ushering, ministry to children, youth, women, or men—it is imperative that you have their blessing so that you can minister with their spiritual covering. It is much easier to use wisdom and godly counsel to be sure of a decision in order to avoid having to backtrack because of a wrong decision. Your decision may deal with your responsibility in your workplace that could lead to a higher position in your job.

If you started at the top with no training, you might find yourself in an insecure place, feeling as though you are standing in midair with no foundation under you. Be sensitive to the doors of opportunity opening for you, and use wisdom in your decisions as you grow and move to your higher position in your workplace or service to the Lord.

> Humility and reverence for the Lord will make you both wise and honored.
>
> —Proverbs 15:33

Do you love Jesus enough to deny yourself the desires of your heart and say, "Lord, I surrender my life to You this day and choose to walk in total submission to Your will for my life."

> Then he said to all, "Anyone who wants to follow me must put aside his own desires and conveniences and carry his cross with him every day and keep close to me!"
> —Luke 9:23

POWER FORCE

I was in a revival service one time, and the church was packed with people. I was alone and sat in the back. When the minister gave the invitation to those that wanted to come up front for prayer, I wanted to go, but since I was alone and there were a lot of people there that I didn't know, I didn't want to leave my purse on the bench unattended. I don't know why I didn't think to take it along with me to the front, but in my carnal mind I started thinking, "I won't go up front. I will just step out in the aisle and stay near my purse."

There were so many going forward that I was forced up front. Some were already there around the altar area praying. When I got to the front where the people were praying, I stepped into a swirling power force of God's presence. I physically felt it. It was swirling from up high to the floor, over and through the people standing there praying. I stepped into a powerful *force*. That was an awesome experience that I have never forgotten. I had been concerned with a physical problem that I felt I might need to see a doctor about, but I hadn't told anyone. As I was standing there, the evangelist came and prayed for me. I was healed that night and never had the problem again.

You can feel God's presence everywhere and anywhere, but I felt a mighty force that night as I stepped in among the praying people.

High Places

My grandson was in his bedroom one day and climbed to the top of his dresser. He was playing and pretending to be Superman. He had placed a small, unstable plastic chair on top of the dresser, and suddenly he fell off and broke his arm.

This reminds me of our journey to the high places in our relationship with God. As the Holy Spirit reveals things in your life that hinder you in your spiritual growth, you have to deal with them. When this is revealed to you through a circumstance and you deal with it, you move on to the next level on your way to growing in your spiritual walk. When you are climbing to your high places of development, have your armor on. To avoid a fall and possible spiritual injury, don't forget to guard your backside. Watch for the stumbling blocks that the enemy of your soul tries to put in your way. You might think you are watching out for pitfalls, but the enemy doesn't play safe games. He hits you where you would never expect. You might be surprised thinking that you would ever be tempted in that area or that someone you trust could treat you that way, but he will try everything.

You need to watch and be alert to what attitudes and thoughts you might be entertaining that would open you up to his games. Your responsibility is to think and dwell on Jesus and get into God's holy presence so that His spirit can instruct and cover you. Your thoughts should stay pure and clean. Thoughts and feelings will come, but when something comes up that you do not want there, dismiss it from your mind and get your thoughts and attitudes in control. Keep your spiritual eyes and ears open and alert to everything around.

Then as you let the Holy Spirit lead you into your next step or level of preparation, with God's help you will be ready and willing to deal with whatever might hinder you from going to your *high places* of commitment in the Lord.

LIVING WATER

> He replied, "If you only knew what a wonderful gift God has for you, and who I am, you would ask me for some living water!"
>
> —John 4:10

Have you noticed that when a person is young and innocent, their eyes are bright and clear and they shine with purity? When they get older, if they love the Lord, live their life for Jesus, and keep their heart and mind pure, they still look young. When a person goes the way of the world, gets into drugs, is loose sexually, and uses language speaking of their negative inner thoughts, sometimes their looks deteriorate and they look old at an early age.

I have seen this type of situation change when they say, "Lord, I have tried it my way, and I have failed. Now I want to turn my life over to You, Jesus, and try it Your way." Their countenance changes and they have a new look. Their face shines with the love of the Lord, and they look younger and healthier.

Do you realize what a wonderful gift God has for you and who Jesus really is to you?

When you use water to wash your hands or dishes, it seems a small amount of water makes a lot when you have to clean up a spill.

Let the Holy Spirit's living water fill you up to over-flowing—running over—and see what a wonderful difference it makes in your life.

> To all who mourn in Israel he will give: Beauty for ashes; Joy instead of mourning; Praise instead of heaviness. For God has planted them like strong and graceful oaks for his own glory.
>
> —Isaiah 61:3

Chapter 11

HONOR AND STABILITY

GODLY WOMAN

I WAS CLEANING HOUSE ONE DAY WHEN MY OLDEST SON CAME up and said, "You're a hard working woman, Mom. You're a Proverbs 31 babe!" "Her children shall call her blessed," says Proverbs 31:28 (author's paraphrase). That statement made all the years of hard work worth it. Take courage when it seems no one cares, for one day your son may come up and say, "Mom, you're a Proverbs 31 babe!"

In today's society women are often exploited and, in their own deception, used by Satan to bring down the morals of our nation. Ladies, let's be proud of our godly heritage. Stand up for godly principles and be daughters of our heavenly King.

> If you can find a truly good wife, she is worth more than precious gems! Her husband can trust her, and she will richly satisfy his needs. She will not hinder him, but help him all her life. . . . She is energetic, a hard worker, and watches for bargains . . . . She is a woman of strength and dignity, and has no fear of old age. When she speaks, her words are wise, and kindness is the rule for everything she says. She watches carefully all that goes on throughout her household, and is never lazy. Her children stand and bless her; so does her husband. He praises her with these words: "There are many fine

women in the world, but you are the best of them all!"
Charm can be deceptive and beauty doesn't last, but a
woman who fears and reverences God shall be greatly
praised. Praise her for the many fine things she does.
These good deeds of hers shall bring her honor and
recognition from even the leaders of the nations.

—Proverbs 31:10–12, 17–18, 25–31

You might think, "How can I measure up to those standards?" Think about it a minute; if you really look at the qualities that describe the Proverbs 31 woman, you may do some of the same things she did. Because of the times you live in, maybe not the same way, but the same things.

Her husband trusted her. She won't hinder him, but helps him. She is energetic and a hard worker who watches for bargains. She has strength and dignity, and doesn't fear old age. Her words are wise, and she is kind. She watches her household carefully, and her husband and children bless her.

You may or may not have financial abilities, but perhaps you work hard in your home and job and at keeping your household in order. Are you emotionally supporting your husband in his work and activities? Do you speak words of kindness to your family and people you come in contact with? Do you have strength and dignity and watch for bargains? Do your husband and children bless you by showing and telling you they appreciate you and love you?

If you can, or are striving to measure up to these questions, then ask yourself, "Am I a godly woman? Are my character and morals representing a godly lifestyle?" As you ponder on these things and strive to become the person God wants you to be, remember these words in Psalm 37:23–24:

The steps of good men are directed by the Lord. He delights in each step they take. If they fall it isn't fatal, for the Lord holds them with his hand.

It is an honor to be a godly woman!

Godly Man

But there is one matter I want to remind you about: that a wife is responsible to her husband, her husband is responsible to Christ, and Christ is responsible to God.
—1 Corinthians 11:3

We talk so much about the godly woman, the Proverbs 31 virtuous woman, but we don't hear much about the godly man. Look at a few men in the Bible that loved God and made a mighty impact on the world:

Adam—Created in God's own image (Gen. 1:26)

Enoch—"Walked with God" (Gen. 5:22, NKJV)

Noah—"Found grace in the eyes of the Lord" (Gen. 6:8, NKJV)

Abraham—Father of a nation (Gen. 12:2)

David—Psalmist and king (1 Sam. 23:1; 2 Sam. 2)

Jesus—"Savior of the world" (John 4:42, NKJV)

Paul—"Appointed by God to be Jesus Christ's messenger" (2 Cor. 1:1)

Today's godly man has the responsibility to have his own personal relationship with the Lord so that he can be the spiritual head of his home. His children will love and respect him. His wife will look upon him with respect and honor. He will be a blessing in the house of the Lord. He will inherit the kingdom of God.

> So he returned home to his father. And while he was still a long distance away, his father saw him coming, and was filled with loving pity and ran and embraced him and kissed him.
>
> —Luke 15:20

In this scripture, we see the heart of a father. In his busy schedule, he may not say everything or be everything you would like him to be, but when trouble comes, his father's heart reaches out to you. He has a responsibility to see that his family knows that they have a heavenly Father God who loves them. He loves them—us—so much that He sent His son, Jesus, to Earth to die on a cross so that they can be forgiven their sins, receive His salvation, and have eternal life in heaven with Him.

The father is a stabilizing force that brings the household back to order!

Chapter 12

WOMEN WARRIORS

LOT'S WIFE

THE BIBLE TELLS US ABOUT LOT AND HIS FAMILY, WHO lived in the city of Sodom. The angels came and told Lot to get his relatives and leave the city, and not even to look back. Because of the wickedness of the people, the angles were going to destroy the city, so Lot took his wife and two daughters and left the city. After leaving, Lot's wife looked back. (See Genesis 19:12–17.)

Due to all the talk about Lot's wife, you wonder how she could be a warrior. She may not have been a warrior; but what she did taught us *not* to disobey what God tells us to do. She had the opportunity to be a good soldier, but she chose the wrong path.

Don't look back to what you thought were pleasures of sin. Sin ultimately leads to destruction. The angels told Lot to take his wife and two daughters and get out of the city, and told them not to look back. Lot's wife disobeyed and turned into a pillar of salt. She didn't know that through the years people would be reading about her and that she would become well known throughout the world. She had the opportunity to be saved and continue life in a different city, but she disobeyed what God told her to do. And because of this, she perished. All through the ages, people have read about her disobedience.

It makes you feel sad when you think about her decision, but you have the opportunity to make your own decision: accept Jesus as your Savior and be saved. Then look at yourself and make the choice to trust and obey God for your life. In your circumstances, there may have been times when you have had to give up something that was very dear to you—a home, job, or marriage. As you look back, you can look with a longing and not be able to lay it down. If you don't let go of it, it can make you bitter or resentful. If you don't deal with it, continuing to hold onto the bitterness and resentment, it can even turn into rebellion, and your whole future can be affected.

You are in a spiritual war. There is an enemy out there that is trying to destroy your soul. Remember Lot's wife and what happened when she looked back. Choose to obey God and walk in the plans that He has for you. Get your eyes off the negative, then you can see beyond the hurt and disappointment and see hope for your future.

Look to God, knowing He cares for you. But you have to trust Him and lay down the good and bad. Let Him heal your hurts and trust Him for a successful future. Then you can become a warrior and help others to overcome by laying down their disappointment and allowing God to heal their battle wounds. You will be remembered as a good soldier that endured to victory!

JOB'S WIFE

Job [was] a good man, who feared God and stayed away from evil. He had a large family of seven sons and three daughters, and was immensely wealthy.

—Job 1:1–2

When Job was tested, he lost all he had—his wealth, his servants, and his children. That means that his wife lost everything, too—her wealth, her servants, her children, and her husband became ill.

In her time of trouble, she even said to Job, "Are you still trying to be godly when God has done all this to you? Curse him and die" (Job 2:9).

She had to walk through her circumstance without knowing the end result. We see the other side of her situation and see the blessing at the end.

If she could only have known the future for her family, maybe she would have been strength to her husband and had more courage to endure. Through all his tragedy and suffering, even though he became discouraged and endured his wife and friends saying discouraging things to him, Job stayed faithful.

After his time of testing was over, the Lord blessed Job with more than he had in the beginning. He had seven more sons and three more daughters. As her husband was restored, so was she—to her wealth, her children, and a healthy husband. "And in all the land there were no other girls as lovely as the daughters of Job," it says of her offspring (Job 42:15).

When the hard times were over, she had a healthy, wealthy man.

You may feel at times that life is hard. I am not referring to situations that are not godly. Job was a good man who feared God and stayed away from evil. But if you recognize that God is allowing you to go through a test and you know that you have a good spouse that is going through an ordeal, respect and keep faith in that person so that both of you can learn and develop in the Lord.

You need to evaluate the situation in love. Ask God for strength and guidance to stand and for godly wisdom in handling your part in the situation. Then when you have come through and are on the other side of the problem, you won't have regrets and have to feel sorry and remorseful about your behavior.

Sometimes in the growing time you get discouraged and may want to give up, but God never fails you. If you walk away, you might abort God's plan for your life.

Learn, and remember Job's wife. Don't come against your husband in a time of testing. Listen to your husband and respect his advice and counsel. He won't always be down; he will arise out of his trouble.

Remember, "Weeping may go on all night, but in the morning, there is joy" (Ps. 30:5).

God rewards faithfulness when you endure to the end.

THE WIDOW WOMAN

First Kings 17:8–16 tells about Elijah and God's provision for the widow of Zarephath:

> Then the Lord said to him, "Go and live in the village of Zarephath, near the city of Sidon. There is a widow there who will feed you. I have given her my instructions." So he went to Zarephath. As he arrived at the gates of the city he saw a widow gathering sticks; and he asked her for a cup of water. As she was going to get it, he called to her, "Bring me a bite of bread, too." But she said, "I swear by the Lord your God that I haven't a single piece of bread in the house. And I have only a handful of flour left and a little cooking oil in the bottom of the jar. I was just gathering a few sticks to cook this last meal, and then my son and I must die of

starvation." But Elijah said to her, "Don't be afraid! Go ahead and cook that 'last meal,' but bake me a little loaf of bread first; and afterwards there will still be enough food for you and your son. For the Lord God of Israel says that there will always be plenty of flour and oil left in your containers until the time when the Lord sends rain, and the crops grow again!" So she did as Elijah said, and she and Elijah and her son continued to eat from her supply of flour and oil as long as it was needed. For no matter how much they used, there was always plenty left in the containers, just as the Lord had promised through Elijah!

The widow had previous instructions from God and knew that Elijah was a man of God. She knew he heard God, so she obeyed. This is a good example of what can happen and how your life can be affected when you trust God and obey what He tells you to do.

Obedience and faith in God's Word are powerful keys for your life. Hear and recognize the Word of the Lord and then be obedient to what He tells you. You must be sensitive to His Holy Spirit, so that you will recognize the voice of the Lord and not be deceived.

Your call may be to serve in some area. Stop and think about it; look at the reward she received for her obedience in her place of serving. The man of God was provided for, and she was rewarded with provision for herself and her family.

RUTH

This is a story about a family that left Israel and went to the land of Moab due to a famine. While they were there, the two sons married girls from Moab. Naomi's husband and two sons died, and Naomi decided to return to Israel. Her daughter-in-law, Ruth, promised to leave her own people in order to stay with Naomi.

> But Ruth replied, "Don't make me leave you, for I want to go wherever you go, and to live wherever you live; your people shall be my people, and your God shall be my God; I want to die where you die, and be buried there. May the Lord do terrible things to me if I allow anything but death to separate us."
>
> —Ruth 1:16–17

The story of Ruth is a beautiful story. It portrays love, faithfulness, and trust in God. Ruth was faithful to her mother-in-law, Naomi, and her mother-in-law's God. She gave up her family, land, and religion—everything—to commit to her mother-in-law, her family, her land, and her God.

She did not have false pride. Her attitude was right when she had to help support herself and Naomi, and she was diligent in working in the fields with her hands. By submitting totally, she later gained a wealthy husband, Boaz, and through her descendants King Jesus was born.

You might say, "How was she a warrior?" We think of a warrior as someone that fights the battle in the field. But some of the most powerful battles are won in the prayer closet. You have to do your part in your job, whatever responsibility it may require of you. Love and counsel your family in the areas that you can to help them. Then totally commit your life, your children, your problems—whatever your battles are—to the Lord. Pray and trust God, knowing He has only your best interest at heart. After you have done all you know to do, leave all your concerns at the feet of Jesus—in your prayer closet.

Trust God that the battle is won and your enemy is defeated. Believe that victory is yours!

PETER'S MOTHER-IN-LAW

Peter was one of Jesus' disciples. His mother-in-law, like some other women in the Bible, isn't named in the Scriptures. However, what happened to her was significant enough to be recorded in history:

> When Jesus arrived at Peter's house, Peter's mother-in-law was in bed with a high fever. But when Jesus touched her hand, the fever left her; and she got up and prepared a meal for them.
>
> —Matthew 8:14–15

Can you imagine Jesus coming to your house in person and touching your hand? Then you get up—well—and fix a meal for Him and those with Him. What an honor! She was faithful, not knowing she would be read about and talked about in our day. She was a servant. She took care of her son-in-law and the men of God who were with him, including Jesus.

You may not be chosen to serve the leaders of ministry in person, but you can pray for them and keep their names lifted up before the Lord. They are called to be at their place in the kingdom, and you are called to your place. Standing in the gap and interceding for others is a high calling.

Your own spouse or sons and daughters may be the men or women of God you are responsible for. God places treasures in your own home to be nourished and protected for the call on their lives. You have a great responsibility in birthing and raising your children. You don't know what greatness God has put in them. Do your part by raising them up to love and serve God, and He will develop the call and anointing that He has placed in them. Don't ever give up on them. Love them and always be there for them.

You and God may be the only ones that know how much you give. The person may or may not know, but God is the one that rewards those that diligently seek Him. (See Hebrews 11:6.) Peter's mother-in-law served without expecting accolades or recognition, but served in her place of responsibility as it came her way.

Healing is for you, too. He is here right now for you.

Jesus Christ is the same yesterday, today, and forever.
—Hebrews 13:8

MY MOTHER

My mother was a grassroots warrior. She was not raised up to affect the world herself, but she raised eight children to love and walk in the ways of the Lord. Even with eight children, she always had a clean house, clean clothes, and food on the table. She and my dad saw that we were taken to church faithfully. She was an honest, quiet, stable lady, solid in her relationship with the Lord, her husband, and her children, and she served them faithfully. I can remember as a child how, after we were in bed, sometimes she would stay up sewing for us.

Now my husband and I are serving the Lord. Her faithfulness in seeing that my siblings and I were raised in the Lord has brought forth seed for the kingdom beyond what she could have expected when she was raising us. She was just being faithful and loving in the responsibilities that came into her life. I can still remember her banana pudding and the other good desserts and meals that she prepared for our family.

As a teenager, I was reading the Bible through. I remember one evening sitting on a stool in the kitchen and reading out loud to her as she prepared dinner. She was so patient.

My mother was a quiet woman and didn't say much. Even though there were hardships in her life at times, there were also a lot of good times and laughter. Every one of her eight children knew without a doubt that we were very important, as well as what was happening in our lives. We knew we were loved individually.

My mother is now home with the Lord, and all of her children have their own families that know and love the Lord. Her grandchildren are carrying on the godly heritage that she handed down to her children, and those grandchildren are handing this same godly heritage down to their children—generation after generation.

There are many of you that are grassroots warriors like my mother; your job or ministry is not to do mighty exploits in the world, but to look after your own family. If your children are grown or you are a grandmother, you still have an effect on your family. The seeds of a godly heritage that you have planted in your children are now being handed down to the next generation of sons and daughters or grandchildren, and you don't know what effect they may have on the world for God.

Thank you Lord, for godly mothers!

My Mother-in-Law

Years ago, my mother-in-law went to a ladies' church function where they were each to bring a dessert. For her contribution, she baked a homemade pie. She didn't drive, so two of the ladies picked her up. One of the ladies had not brought anything, so they stopped at a little coffee and soda fountain place that served pie. The lady had to buy a pie that was missing a piece because the restaurant didn't have any whole ones. Upon arriving at their destination, the lady took in the pie that my mother-in-law had made, leaving her to carry in the partial one. She was sweet and gracious and didn't say a word. By quietly going in and setting the pie down, no one thought much about my mother-in-law; but if she had made a scene, she would have made herself and the lady who drove her to the event look bad.

The rewards of humility are much greater than the accolades you might get from any culinary achievement. It takes a strong, courageous, and mature person with a pure heart to face embarrassing situations that you didn't expect or deserve. By guarding your mouth and your behavior, you can lift your head up high with a pure heart that has no anger and no bitter words dripping from your lips.

God sees your reactions and behavior. He loves you, and He cares about the smallest things that happen to you. In time He will reward you in a much greater way than you could ever imagine. Going through the fires of preparation makes you mature, so that when situations arise that you do not expect, you won't get into an emotional upheaval. You will respond with dignity and grace that will make you feel good about yourself and earn the respect of others.

Chapter 13

LOVE, MAINTENANCE, AND SPIRITUAL GROWTH

FOR ALL YOUR WELDING NEEDS

I WAS GOING DOWN THE ROAD ONE DAY AND AS I PASSED A building, there was a sign that read "For all your welding needs." At first I misread the sign and thought it said, "For all your *wedding* needs." I thought about it and realized that there is some similarity in the meaning of those two words.

A marriage needs to be welded together at times by the presence and intervention of God's Spirit. When a metal part is cracked or broken and needs repair, you go to a welder or get a welder's torch and merge the metal together to seal the cracked or broken piece.

When you have relationships, either with friends or in the context of marriage, there will be times when you feel the strain of the hardship life brings your way. This is why you need to include God's Holy Spirit in the very beginning of relationships. With His love and peace, it is easier to go through the struggles and storms of life that may come your way.

If you find you have not included Him, it is not too late to ask Him to come in and heal the cracked or broken pieces of your life so that your hearts can be mended and merged together again.

Keep a daily maintenance on your relationship so that you can recognize a need before it gets broken and has to be repaired. Keep God's Holy Spirit, the master welder, there so that your life and situations will stay strong in Him.

HE IS CHRISTMAS

> For there is born to you this day in the city of David a Savior, who is Christ the Lord.
>
> —Luke 2:11, NKJV

I wrote the following article a few years ago and sent it to my hometown newspaper. They put it in the Letters to the Editor section on Christmas Eve. It was the only article for that day. Even though it was written years ago, the profound message is still the same. He is *still* the Savior of the world. How can they take Him out of Christmas? He is Christmas!

> Glory to God in the highest, And on earth peace, good-will toward men!
>
> —Luke 2:14, NKJV

Almost everyone anticipates the time of year when we celebrate Christmas. This day we wish love, peace, and good cheer to friends, loved ones, and our fellowman.

A few years ago, I saw a program on television where the evil magician kidnapped Santa Claus and tried to take over the world and steal Christmas. This was an interesting story. Evil and selfishness were replacing the spirit of Christmas.

Then we have Christ. This is the one very special day we celebrate His birth. He came from heaven and took His place as a baby born in a lowly place, among the cattle and sheep. In a manger the Christ Child was placed. (See Luke 2:6–7.) He came to give us His love, peace, and joy that we may have if we believe and accept Him. But we have evil trying to take Him away from us. There are those that want to take Him out of schools, out of everything; the only thing that brings real peace, love, and joy.

How can they take Him out of Christmas? He is Christmas![1]

WALKING THE WALK IN A REAL WORLD

Many times with all sincerity, we say things like; "Change my heart, Lord," or, "I want to be like Jesus." We make these statements without understanding the magnitude of what we are saying.

You may have accepted Jesus as your Savior and received forgiveness for your sins, but you want a deeper relationship with the Lord. As you read the Bible and pray, you find that you have a desire to go to the deeper places in the spirit that are available to anyone that has a heart and desire to know His presence in a more personal way. You say, "Yes, I want to, but how can I do this? How can I know Jesus better and experience God's Holy Spirit in a more intimate way?"

He desires to draw closer to you and wants you to know Him better, but you have to seek Him in your prayer closet and worship and praise Him. Tell Him how you feel. Tell Him you love Him and desire His presence in your life. Then as you talk to Him and you feel the sweet presence of God rising up inside you, enjoy His presence, love Him, and worship Him. But there is a time when you need to be quiet and listen to His voice. Let God's Holy Spirit speak to your spirit as He draws you into the deeper places that you can go in Him. Let Him show you that He loves you and desires to be your friend and to have fellowship and communion with you.

After you have developed in your personal relationship and intimate walk with the Lord, you may desire to serve Him and lead others into salvation or a deeper experience in their Christian walk. Then you may have a sincere desire to be more like Jesus. To be like Jesus, you have to be willing to let the Holy Spirit of God expose and purify things in you that you may need to give up or change.

This willingness consists of making the decision to allow the Holy Spirit to purge from within you things that you don't want there, such as wrong attitudes or behavior that you may not know are there or don't know what to do about them. The Lord will reveal these negative attitudes or behaviors to you through situations that bring those attitudes to the surface.

When I was young, I used to look up in prayer and talk to the Lord saying, "Lord, when people look at me, I don't want them to see me; I want them to see Jesus." As time passed and I went through different situations and circumstances on my road in developing in my Christian walk, I learned that you don't become like Jesus just because your heart desires it in all purity and sincerity. There has to be a total transformation of your heart and attitude. To be like Jesus, you will not only have God's love flowing through you, but you will also have to be a partaker in His suffering and sorrow. There are heart-wrenching experiences you may have to go through. Jesus had to go to the cross in His walking the walk in a real world. His walk was not a walk of glory and recognition, but a walk of persecution and rejection—even by His best friends, who did not understand the magnitude of what was happening. They may not have known that He was the true

Son of God that had come to Earth to bring salvation to a lost and dying world. Do you think Peter would have denied Jesus if he had known that, all the way down through the years of time, you and I would be touched and influenced by his life as we read the Bible?

The followers of Christ walked their walk in a real world, just as you and I, not knowing that the recognition and fame comes after the purging and cleansing of our heart. After your heart is truly purged and you are walking in the fullness of God's Spirit, you won't want any glory; all the glory belongs to Jesus. He made it all possible for you. You will just want to walk among His people and see lives changed. You say, "My life has been changed." This is true, you will change when you have had a divine encounter with the Lord of your life and you let the Holy Spirit have total control. You will not think and do the things you used to do. You will have compassion for others. God is looking for a heart change.

Second Chronicles 16:9 (NKJV) says:

> For the eyes of the Lord run to and fro throughout the whole earth, to show Himself strong on behalf of those whose heart is loyal to Him.

He is looking for people whose heart is loyal to Him and for people who are willing to go through whatever it takes to commit to a life of becoming like Jesus. When you are a willing person for Him to use, He can trust you not to break and turn away in the preparation times that you may go through. During these times, when you feel you have gone your limit and cannot go another step, you think, "Where could I go? Jesus, You are the only Way. There is nothing without You." Things may get tough, and it is then that you have to watch your heart and attitude.

You may go through trials and you may get tired and frustrated, but God is watching your heart and attitude. Even if you're angry, is your heart staying pure? You ask, "How can my heart stay pure if I am angry?" The Bible says, "Be angry, and do not sin" (Eph. 4:26, NKJV). You will have the emotional feeling; but what you have to watch out for is that you don't dwell on the situation so much that it causes hate or bitterness to enter into your heart. You may go through a situation sometime that will be devastating to you, and you have wrong feelings trying to enter. I am referring to the emotions that happen to you that you have to deal with in order to have a pure heart.

Growing to a different level may cause situations to rise up and emotions arise in you that you may not have ever experienced before. Then you have the choice of harboring those emotions—maybe causing you to do something you would be sorry for later or saying something you could never retrieve. In your prayer time, you may realize that wrong feelings or hurts were trying to enter your heart. Even though you may be an easygoing person and get over things easily, you may recognize emotions that you have not felt before. As you deal with them (it may take a few days), you don't like the feelings they are causing you to have in your heart. You know that you cannot harbor those feelings, and you have a desire to be rid of that particular emotion that is trying to enter. Through prayer and love of Jesus, you can get the victory over the situation and deal with the feelings that were trying to enter. As you mature in your walk with the Lord, you learn to control your emotions, not let them control you.

As you experience things that cause you to grow in your walk with the Lord, the experiences you go through help you spiritually so that you will not be gullible in some areas.

Going through situations that bring you to a higher spiritual level brings out things in you. These may not be feelings rooted in you and you may not have to deal with your heart, but they may show you some things. If other people are involved, you need to be able to recognize the response in others so you won't be deceived. But you will have to deal with the emotions that arose in you over the situation.

There may be different kinds of sorrow and emotions you may feel and have to deal with as you partake of the suffering and sorrow of Jesus. They cannot stay; they must be dealt with. I have found that, although the two are intertwined, growth comes from experience. When you get saved, you are a child of God, but you still need to be transformed. There are things in your life you have to become aware of and ask God to change in you (such as pride, jealousy, anger, fear, selfishness, greed, etc.). Things will happen to bring these underlying things to the surface so that you realize they are there. For instance, if you have pride, a situation will arise to bring that pride to your attention. You will feel so ashamed of the way you behaved, not because of something someone else did or said to you, but by the Holy Spirit exposing it to you. You then realize, "My goodness! That pride has to go!" Don't let shame linger, or it could cause you a problem. Just humble yourself before the Lord, and let the presence of His sweet Holy Spirit heal you.

One time I was in a place where I had recognition from a person that I felt had a prestigious position. I was in a church meeting, and at the invitation to come forward to commit to something that I was moved by, I went up front and stood among the others. While standing there, this person came and stood beside me and put her arm around my waist. We stood there listening to the speaker. I felt so exalted because this lady was giving me so much attention. When I got home, I looked in the mirror. I don't know how, but somehow I had managed to wipe the lipstick off one total half (top and bottom) of the right side of my mouth. The left side of the mouth had lipstick on; the right side had none. I looked at myself and laughed. I said, "OK, there goes the pride." I still laugh when I think about it. There I was in front of everyone with half a mouth. This incident revealed the pride in me. Dealing with situations in your life may be an ongoing process. Sometimes it may bring laughter, and sometimes it may cause tears. But whatever you go through, let the love of Jesus see you all the way through.

If you have fear, something will happen to make you declare, "God, I need you to deliver me from fear." Everyone gets scared at times, but if it is more often than that, these are things in you that you have to deal with for your peace of mind and spiritual growth.

Heart sorrow is a deep sorrow that someone else causes. Things inside of another person may come forth to hurt and harass you. You need to deal with your emotions, but still maintain a godly love for them. You may not like them, but don't let sin enter your heart. Someday if you haven't dealt with these emotions, you may stand before Jesus with wrong feelings and thoughts in your heart. It takes a strong commitment to God to be willing to say, "Lord, I don't like this, but keep my heart pure before You and let Your love flow through me."

There are a lot of different emotions you may go through as you are walking the walk in a real world, but as Paul says in Philippians 3:13–14:

> No, dear brothers, I am still not all I should be but I
> am bringing all my energies to bear on this one thing:

Forgetting the past and looking forward to what lies
ahead, I strain to reach the end of the race and receive
the prize for which God is calling us up to heaven
because of what Christ Jesus did for us.

STEP BY STEP

In your preparation for walking the walk in a real world,
don't be gullible and follow wrong voices. As you develop
in your relationship with the Lord and deal with the issues
in your life that the Holy Spirit has exposed to you, you will
move to a higher level or higher place in your Christian walk.
I did not understand this at first, but learned as I grew in my
knowledge of the things of God.

There will be a lot of well-meaning people that either
haven't been called to the walk you have or that were called
and did not respond. Maybe they weren't willing to pay the
price, but they will want to offer their advice. Be courteous.
They may have a word of wisdom, but don't be gullible and
follow wrong advice. Get in your prayer closet, seek the face
of God, and follow His voice.

If you feel you do not understand what is happening to
you and need advice, go to your pastor or someone that you
know will give you godly advice, not just their opinion. Love
everyone, but don't receive someone as on your spiritual
level when he or she has not paid the price to be there. You
will recognize this as you grow in your own walk. They may
either hurt you, or they could be hurt that you don't take
their advice. This does not mean you are walking in pride,
but rather that they may be on another level and may not
understand where you are walking. They may be moving and
talking in their intellect, not the Spirit, and may not have
comprehension of where you are spiritually. They may talk a

good line, thinking they know what you know, when they do not understand. This could discourage you. If you open yourself up to share with them on a level they are not prepared for, they may repeat what you say to others and cause you much pain. If you are walking where you should be with the Lord, you won't be saying anything intentionally that would hurt others, though they may misunderstand your intentions.

Others may walk on your level for awhile, then the enemy may come along with a hard knock in their life that they may not be prepared to deal with. When you are moving from level to level, the higher you go, the harder the devil tries to discourage and stop you. If someone is trying to walk with you and has not gone through the preparation levels you have, they may not be ready for the intense spiritual battle that you may be going through at the time, and they could be hurt spiritually.

When you are at each level, God prepares you to go higher and higher. You are not ready for the high level of testing until you have gone through the step-by-step levels that He takes you through. Everyone has different giftings and calling, so each person has their own place of preparation they may have to walk through. If someone skips their preparation, which may not be the same as yours, they may not be ready for the battle you are experiencing on your level. It doesn't mean you are better or higher than them, just that you are on a different level and experience of preparation. Do not judge anyone. Keep your heart pure before the Lord and watch others' attitudes and spiritual fruit. Let the Holy Spirit lead you in your relationships.

There may be those that try to glean from your experience, then walk away from you, causing you hurt because you thought they were your friend. Don't be discouraged.

You will go through a lot of experiences and a lot of people will walk through your life. Some may stay, but others will walk through, receiving what God has for them to receive from you. Touch the ones God sends and love all of them.

In the story of Joseph, God gave Joseph dreams about His plan for his life. Joseph shared these dreams, and was thrown into a pit. (See Genesis 37.)

We all have visions and dreams of our own that we would like to come to pass. Sometimes these are our own ideas, not God's plan for us. He always has much better plans for us than we could ever imagine. But when God gives you words or dreams about your life and promises of His plans for you, it is so exciting that you want to run and tell everyone. It is all right to share some things with others, but there are times when you need to really hear God and know for sure that it is all right to share what He has given you.

You have to be careful what you share. If the person you share with is not ready to receive what has been revealed to you, you can cause a delay in God's plan—or even be thrown in a metaphorical pit, taking years for the dreams to come to pass while you are stuck in a place of waiting and holding. If others involved don't receive, it may change things, but if you are faithful to what God is saying to you, He will use you in other ways.

Sometimes you don't quite understand what He is saying, and you may interpret things in your own understanding, which may not be exactly what He is saying. Your plan may have looked more exciting and glorious, but God's plan for your life is exciting—whatever path it may take you. When things get tough, keep your eyes on Jesus and your ears tuned into what the Holy Spirit is saying, and He will direct your path, each step of the way. Even though you may have to walk through deep waters in life before His plan comes to fruition, submit to His will. Remember, His plans are good plans for you.

The training you are receiving by going through situations not only makes you have a more intimate relationship with God, but it also prepares you for an anointed, powerful ministry to bring help and deliverance to others. If you did not experience things, how could you understand or comprehend what others are going through? If you do not have a personal, tried-and-proven relationship with God, how can you tell others with authority that God loves them and wants to change their lives?

A baby can bring joy and laughter to you, but cannot heal your hurt. They have to grow up and learn about life before they can bring wisdom and understanding to your life. So it is with you as a Christian. You can enjoy others and bring them joy and laughter, but when they need someone to help bring them out of a tough situation, they need someone who can deal with the real world—not religiously, but in reality understanding where they are walking. Some are walking in tough places, and it may take a tried-by-fire person to be able to bring them hope.

Just as the rain comes to water the earth and the sun shines to bring health to our trees, flowers, and plants, the rain must come into your life. It seems like it hinders you at times, but it helps you to grow and mature. Then God's "Sonlight" shines upon you to bring health for your spiritual growth. God loves you, and He only wants good for you. But in order for you to grow, the rain (and sometimes storms) have to come. They have their purpose. However, just as surely as the rain comes, the sun will shine and there will be beautiful, colorful rainbows in your life.

DECISION/INDECISION

When you have made the decision to follow Jesus, you feel that you have been called to a higher place in your walk with the Lord, and you have a desire and longing for a deeper and more intimate relationship with Him, there may be decisions to make. You see, as you grow in the Lord, you move to levels of maturity in your Christian walk. You can choose to stay at any level, or you can say, "Lord, I want to go to higher levels or places in my relationship with You."

For years I was content in the place where I was in my relationship with the Lord. But there came a time when I started realizing that there was a higher and more intimate place that I could obtain. When I started realizing this, I had a desire to go to that deeper place in God's presence.

When I was developing in my spiritual walk, I didn't understand what was happening to me. But since then I have learned that I was growing and maturing. Perhaps you feel you have experienced changes and purging in areas of your life, but you feel like you are still in a place of changing as new things are brought to the surface. You see, when you get to the top of one level, it also means you are at the bottom of your next level. You have been purged and developed at that level and have grown into a higher place. You will feel that you have changed and things are different, but you may not understand the feelings you are experiencing. God is omnipotent, so if you are willing, you still have higher places to go and other things in your life you may need to deal with.

Decisions are a choice of the mind, but the heart also must be involved when committing totally to the Lord and choosing to say, "I am willing, Lord. I am one You can count on—one who will allow You to take me to the higher places in You where You desire for me to go." When you make this decision mentally, there is definitely a process your heart must go through in order to commit fully to the Lord. As time goes by and you experience some heart-wrenching circumstances and situations to purge and purify you, you may think, "Lord, I don't know if I can handle anymore." Again, each mental decision to commit your life to Him will take your heart into a deeper place of surrender to the Lord.

You see, the higher the levels you go in your commitment, the purer you have to be. You can't get away with the things you did when you were on a different level. People will be watching you, and the least little spot will be very obvious. My husband shared with me that when you are developing in your relationship with the Lord, you are like a spot on a sheet. If the sheet is very colorful with print, a black spot is not too noticeable, but a black spot on a white sheet is very noticeable. As your heart is being purged, a spot in your life is more noticeable to others. You will never be perfect, but you will improve in your actions and attitudes as you get more and more intimate with the Holy Spirit.

You have to watch your language. Anger has to be very controlled. Your attitudes will have to stay in check, and you can't let just anyone see your imperfections. They may not be able to handle it because they expect so much more out of you.

The secret is to always be real. Don't put on a false image; then they won't be shocked when they see you as a human, with human feelings and reactions. What helps you to handle this type of scrutiny is the knowledge that as you go to the higher levels and your heart is getting purged, the things that make you react are being purified, and you are less likely to react in an unseemly way. I am not saying you won't. I am saying you will be less likely to do so, if you have dealt with the attitude in your heart that would cause you to react in the wrong way. Sometimes frustration, not sin, causes the wrong thought and actions to come forth. When this happens, it shows you that you may need to trust God more and there may still be areas that need to be dealt with.

Ask God for daily strength to carry you through each day as you, in your willing heart, allow Him to purify you to help you become like Jesus. Make a decision: "With your help Lord, I want to continue my walk in becoming like Jesus."

The rewards are great when you persevere all the way through your trial or situation. You will see family members change, lives healed and touched, and your own circumstances will get better. It is worth it all. It may be heart-wrenching at times, and you may feel shame or hurt as you deal with your inner emotions and problems. However, the end result from each trial will bring joy and a great feeling of accomplishment when you see what God did for you because you endured.

If you are in a place of indecision, think about the consequences. Your life may be affected in your decision to go on with the Lord or to stay at the level you are at presently.

Genesis 11:31 (NKJV) says:

> And Terah took his son Abram and his grandson Lot, the son of Haran, and his daughter-in-law Sarai, his son Abram's wife, and they went out with them from Ur of the Chaldeans to go to the land of Canaan; and they came to Haran and dwelt there.

They were on their way to the Promised Land, but they stopped before they got there. It may have been a good place, but it was not the Promised Land. You have the choice of staying at your place of indecision or saying:

God, I do want to go all the way to Your promised land for me. But I will need Your supernatural strength and determination to go to the next level. I choose to make the decision to follow You all the way. And Lord, help me to hear Your voice and not get deceived by the wrong voice that would lead me astray. I know You have good things planned for me, and You will not take me to a hard place that will lead to my destruction. But You will take me to a good place where I will grow and be nourished by Your Spirit.

When God is allowing you to go through things to mature and develop you, you may have to face them alone, just you and God. If you can share your decision with family or a close friend and they understand and have the knowledge revealed to them about what is happening, they may be able to stand with you and not add to your problems. When God is purging you, He is showing you your own heart and attitudes. He is not showing you another person's problems. He is dealing with you and your relationship with Him. If things get too hard and are causing you stress, you need to make sure you are not making decisions on your own. When God is showing you areas in your life that you need to deal with, it is a joy because as He purges you, you reach out to Him and He is also there reaching out to and loving you. You need not have a sad, sorrowful face, but a happy face. As you allow Him to show you things you need to deal with, sometimes you might feel like breaking and running away saying, "God, I can't take it anymore." But the joy on the other side brings healing, restoration, and rejoicing. Then when you look at yourself after some purging and see how far you came, you'll have a totally different outlook about your life. You'll also see others more maturely. You will see their human faults but still know God is working on them, too. He is looking for people that will allow Him to take them through some hard places of purging and come out with anointing power and the fire of God in their bones, so that they can minister healing and deliverance to others in need of His touch.

There is a time when God requires you to be at a certain place in Him, but there are also times when He releases you to let you walk in your desired place. Remember as you strive to be more like Jesus not to neglect your family. Always look after your family. They are your God-given responsibility. Love them and do all you can to teach them in the ways of the Lord.

> Train up a child in the way he should go, And when he is old he will not depart from it.
> —Proverbs 22:6, NKJV

When you feel the presence of the Holy Spirit drawing you aside, it will not conflict with your responsibility to your family. Be open and sensitive to hear His voice and feel His spirit drawing you to that quiet place of worship with Him.

If you feel you have been going back and forth trying to find the place where you belong in your walk with the Lord, seek God for direction. Direction in your life brings peace.

The Lord loves you. Go in peace on your way to becoming more and more like Jesus.

THANK YOU FOR TRUSTING ME

Lord, my soul cries out to You. Make me pure and holy in Your sight. I want to be Your servant and to please You. I am willing to go through the purging and testing in my life, but Holy Spirit, I need You to stay close to me. I know You are there. You will never leave or forsake me, but Holy Spirit, let me feel You are there. Let me feel Your sweet, holy presence that comforts, strengthens, and sustains me. Then Lord, when my testing and development at this level or season of time in my life is over, let me bask in the glorious exhilaration of the freedom of peace that helps me to know that each testing time is temporary. You are developing and preparing me to be your servant, so that I may be a blessing to others to help them learn and grow in You, to help them learn and understand how to help others that are going through trials. As we grow and develop and learn to put our faith and trust in You, when we speak over people, our prayers will have power to bring healing and restoration. Through it all, we will win souls for Your kingdom. Thank You for trusting me enough to choose me. Now, give me the strength and courage to endure, knowing that when each trial is over, I become more and more like Jesus.

Chapter 14

EMOTIONS, MERCY, AND GRACE

CONFUSION

CONFUSION OF THE MIND AND CONFUSED TIMES IN YOUR life are two separate things. What we may think is mind confusion is really our attempt at dealing with areas of the heart. Even though thought process is involved, the mind itself is clear. What we feel is the emotion of not understanding a situation.

One time my husband and I were taking a faith walk and trusting God in all areas of our life. We needed new tires for our car. When you have finances, you don't even need to think about it; you just go out and buy a new set of tires. If you can take care of it, I believe God expects you to do so, but there are times when you are in circumstances that won't allow you to do that. So at this season in our life, we didn't have the finances to buy them.

I was traveling home from work one day on an interstate highway and had a flat tire. Since we were trusting Him, I questioned why God allowed me to have a flat tire on an interstate highway. I probably would have been safer to drive on the flat and try to get to an exit; but when things happen, you make decisions at the moment that you think are best. I pulled over to the side of the road and said, "God, you said you would take care of us, and look at me. Here I sit." Cars were passing so fast that it was scary to even try to open the door. I sat there a few minutes with cars zipping on by, no one seeming to care. While I sat there feeling sorry for myself and questioning the situation I was in, no one stopped. Finally, I carefully opened the door and got out to look at my situation. After I made the move, while I was looking at the tire, two separate vehicles stopped—so quickly that I didn't even see them stop or the men get out of their vehicles. One stopped in front of my car, the other behind me. I soon had two guys changing my tire. I didn't get any results as long as I was sitting and complaining. But when I made a move, help came. I realize there are times when you can't do anything, when all you can do is stay put and trust God, but in this particular situation I felt that I had to make a move. When you are in a dangerous circumstance, you need to tune in your spiritual ears so that you can hear God's voice to know when to move and when to stay put.

Things may be going by in your life so fast that you can't step out of your situation at first, and you may feel that no one cares what is going on. God cares. My husband shares:

> Do not allow your circumstance and your situations
> to separate you from God's presence. Don't look at the
> storm, the wind, and waves that cause you to be afraid.
> God is able to change your circumstance and situa-
> tions. He is your waymaker where there seems to be no
> way. He desires to bless you and turn your dark nights
> to overcoming days of victory over all your troubles.
> Allow Him to gather you to Himself beneath the safety
> of His wings. (See Psalm 57:1.) Just look to Him, call
> on Him, worship Him, and praise Him, and He will
> manifest Himself and His glory to you. He will stir up
> your still, cold waters and cause them to flow again in

Emotions, Mercy, and Grace

joy and strength. He will deliver and enable you, and bring overcoming victory to your life.

Just as in the situation with my car, God provided me with two young, strong men to change my tire. I believe He will bless the men for helping me. He blessed me by keeping me safe when the tire went flat while I was driving by, protecting me when I had to get out of the car in a dangerous place, and then by providing the safety of two young men that helped me get out of my dilemma and on my way. If I hadn't had God to call on, they might not have been impressed to stop and help me. Whether they realized it or not, they were used by God to help me. Somewhere down the road God will reward them by sending help to them when they need someone to intervene in their situation.

If you are in a difficult place in your life sometime and confusion is trying to enter, remember: God is a good God who loves and looks after His children. So trust Him and let Him show Himself strong on your behalf.

BITTERNESS

Bitterness, when not dealt-with, can literally make you sick. Bitterness usually comes from being hurt so badly by someone you trusted that you weep for a while and then put up a wall of bitterness to keep anyone from getting near you. This, then, can lead to loneliness. No one will stick around a bitter person too long, because that person can't seem to see beyond their bitterness. They dwell and dwell on it until people grow tired of hearing it. Without people around, you become a very sad person. This can even affect your countenance. If bitterness is not dealt with, your face will begin to sag, your mouth will turn down, your shoulders will slump, and you will look sad and dejected—a smile cannot be found anywhere.

If you find yourself in this situation, please don't coddle it; let bitterness go. It isn't worth it! Don't let your unwillingness to lay down your past cheat you out of your future.

Hebrews 12:15 says:

> Look after each other so that not one of you will fail to find God's best blessings. Watch out that no bitterness takes root among you, for as it springs up it causes deep trouble, hurting many in their spiritual lives.

God bless you. May you be blessed mightily by the presence of God in your life.

ANGER

Sometimes you may hear someone say, "I don't get angry, I just fly off the handle occasionally." The thing about flying off the handle—though it may not be as devastating as anger—is that it can certainly embarrass you and make you look bad. You may say things you will regret and could even possibly abort plans for your life. The Lord impressed to my husband and I early on in our spiritual development, "Guard your mouth and your behavior." (See Psalm 141:3.)

Anger is an emotion that definitely has to be dealt with. If not controlled, it can cause devastating circumstances with heartbreaking results. You may not have the problem that some people have experienced, but if you let anger come between you and loved ones or friends, it can cause hurt and heartbreak, even for years to come.

There are occasions where family members or neighbors have not spoken for a long time because they got angry about something. They may not even remember what the anger was about, but their feelings have gone so deeply that they still have a problem with that person. When this happens to you or someone you know, the solution for this problem is forgiveness. You may say, "This is bigger than forgiveness." No, it is a matter of turning away from it and not holding on to the hurt. First ask God's forgiveness, and then forgive the one that caused you the emotional hurt or anger. You might say, "I just can't forget what they did to me." However, in the prayer closet you *can* deal with your own feelings and forgive. It may take a lot of praying and crying to purge your heart, but if you are sincere, it can be done. Jesus had to forgive. He was treated much worse than you were. He bore the sin of all mankind; you just have to deal with your own. Anger, if not dealt with, can cause hatred. Then a lot of emotional hurt can come to you and others involved in the situation. Let it stop with you; don't hand it down to your future generations.

Let the healing power of Jesus pour over you and bring restoration to your hurting heart. Yes, anger brings hurt to your heart. Only forgiveness brings joy and peace beyond comprehension and understanding.

> And the whole multitude sought to touch Him, for power went out from Him and healed them all.
> —Luke 6:19, NKJV

Rebellion

When you think of rebellion, you think of young, rebellious children or teenagers. However, adults can be just as rebellious. You may not have been a problem child with a rebellious spirit that carried over to adulthood, but we all seem to have that "I want it my way" spirit lurking down inside somewhere.

In marriage, many people think everything must go their way, with no thought of the hardship it is placing on their spouse. They may want to serve God, and will, with all your heart, as long as they are allowed to do what they want and have total control.

When God starts stirring your spirit and nudging you to "come on up higher in Me," the kicking and screaming, "I want it my way," will start, causing you to kick and resist—maybe a little bit, maybe a lot. But if you sincerely mean, "Lord, I want to go to the high places in You," you will have to submit to His will for your life. You may cry and indulge in a little self-pity because you think you will have to give up areas you love and want to cling to. You may be required to give up some habits and behavior if they will hinder you. But God is a gentle God. He will take you at your pace, unless you procrastinate. Then He may squeeze you and prod you with circumstances and situations that will make you bend. Remember that He loves you and only has good planned for your life. It is only you that will hinder that plan, unless you have a willing spirit to let Him mold you into the wonderful person that you can be in Him.

As you let His Holy Spirit purge and cleanse the rebellion out, you will be so thankful, because you will start taking on the character of Christ. You will love the person you are becoming. Even if you have always been a good person and treated everyone well, if you let God develop you to His higher place for you, all those around you will see the change. They will see your godly countenance and be glad.

SELF-PITY

Rebellion is very obnoxious, but self-pity is very repulsive. When you are indulging in self-pity, people will start removing themselves from your presence. It will drive your friends and loved ones away.

People indulging in self-pity won't try to help themselves. Instead, they sit and whine about their situation. Friends and family may be doing everything they can to help and make life better, but it doesn't work. They enjoy having everyone cater to them.

One day people may run out on them, because there is no pleasing a person indulging in self-pity. Everyone feels sorry for him- or herself at times and wishes their circumstances were better, but if you find yourself going into self-pity, take a look around you. It is much more fun when you have a good, happy attitude about yourself and life, and you will attract, not repulse, people. Don't live in a negative state. Indulge in a smile and give a good report. You will feel better. If you need help, ask for it, but be appreciative and thankful.

There are times when frustration may sound like self-pity, but there is a difference. Frustration comes when you have done and tried everything, yet it seems the rocks keep falling on you until finally you say, "I can't take anymore." You are afraid to hope or dream because the hopes and dreams seem to get shattered before they can come to fruition. Don't despair. There is hope. Don't give up on your dreams. God promised He wouldn't give you more than you could bear. Keep trusting Him!

Isaiah 50:7 says:

> Because the Lord God helps me, I will not be dismayed; therefore, I have set my face like flint to do his will, and I know that I will triumph.

FORGIVENESS

> For God did not send his Son into the world to condemn the world, but that the world through him might be saved.
>
> —John 3:17, NKJV

At the end of a service at church one Sunday, the minister gave the opportunity for everyone to come forward to pray. As I was kneeling and praying and talking to the Lord about a tragedy that had happened to my family, I had to confront my emotions.

Emotions can cause you problems when they are not dealt with. I feel that when you have experienced a tragedy along with the sense of loss of a person, you have to deal with wondering where they are and what is happening to them. You may always feel the loss, and, if the tragedy occurred because of another person, you may not feel compassion toward the individual that caused the pain. Nonetheless, you can't let painful emotions, which could cause hate and bitterness to take root in your heart, consume you. For your sake, you need to release them. They are negative emotions that could bring harm to you physically and spiritually. Turn your pain and hurt over to Jesus, who knows and is in control of all things.

It is not easy to face feelings of unforginess. A battle rages in your spirit while you pray and try to make the decision to ask Jesus to save the soul of the other person. Even if you may not have any feelings of forgiveness, you can ask Jesus to save their soul. The devil is out to destroy everyone, but Jesus, in His mercy, rescues you. Jesus died on the cross for everyone.

If you are carrying a heavy load of sorrow in your heart—no matter what caused it—or if you feel that you have caused sorrow to another person, let the mercy and grace of Jesus cover you as you go through this battle to forgive yourself or the person that has caused you great pain. You can do it by God's grace. It forgives and cleanses all of your sins. You can be forgiven for your sins if you repent and recognize Jesus as your Savior. Ask Him to forgive you, change you, and come into your life and be the Lord of it.

If you let Satan control your life, he will take you to the pits. But no matter what you have done, Jesus loves you. Know this: there is an enemy out to destroy you, but Jesus loves you and wants to forgive and draw you to Himself. Then as you are forgiven, you can recognize this and forgive too—not with words or intellect, but from the heart.

The devil is out to destroy, so it is up to you how much you open yourself up to him. Don't play games with your spiritual walk. Stay under God's grace and protective covering. There is a hard way to come to God and there is an easy way—you have the choice. Unforgiveness brings pain and possible devastation to you. Forgiveness brings restoration, peace, and joy in the presence of the Lord.

> If we confess our sins, He is faithful and just to forgive
> us our sins and to cleanse us from all unrighteousness.
> —1 John 1:9, NKJV

As Christians, sometimes we may cause pain to others, too. As we walked with the Lord in the call on our lives, my husband's parents didn't always understand some of the decisions that we made. We didn't know it at the time, but we know now that God had plans for us, and we were being shaken from our nest. His parents didn't realize the call on my husband's life, so they made some decisions that hurt him. After they went to heaven, my husband had a dream in which his mother came to him. She said, "We realize now that we did you a grave injustice, but we had a talk with the Lord. He said, 'Don't worry about him; I am taking care of him.'"

After the dream, he felt better. They know now about the call of God on his life and all the wonderful things the Lord has accomplished through him.

The Bible says in 1 Corinthians 13:12 (NKJV):

> For now we see in a mirror, dimly, but then face to face. Now I know in part, but then I shall know just as I also am known.

Whether you have hurt someone else or they have hurt you, when you get to heaven, you will see and understand all things as things are revealed to you. But if you are hurting now, first ask Jesus to forgive you and then forgive yourself. Then if you feel you may have hurt others or if someone has hurt you, ask Him to forgive you and help you forgive them. When you get to heaven, God will wipe away all tears, but learning to forgive now will bring joy and peace to your life today.

The Bible says in Revelation 21:4 (NKJV):

> And God will wipe away every tear from their eyes; there shall be no more death, nor sorrow, nor crying. There shall be no more pain, for the former things have passed away.

Let the love of Jesus heal your hurting heart and as you are forgiven, then you can forgive others.

SORROW

When you think of the word *sorrow*, it implies some type of sadness that has overtaken you. It could be a very hurtful situation in the family with your children, divorce, illness, or death.

Death is a hard sorrow to have to deal with. Even though the others mentioned are very heart wrenching, there is hope for change. As long as there is life, there is hope. In death, you know it is the end of a way of life. You know if they have accepted Christ, you will see them again, but still there is a deep sorrow that has to be dealt with. Whatever your sorrow that you are dealing with, there is a healthy crying time, but be careful that it doesn't turn into deep, hidden grief.

We are inclined to think the one who doesn't show much emotion isn't taking it very hard. I have learned that isn't always the truth. Some people put their grief way down deep inside, and do not deal with it right away. Eventually you will have to deal with it. The longer you keep it hidden away inside, the harder it is to resolve.

If not dealt-with, sooner or later you will start seeing the results of hidden grief. Your countenance will start taking on a strained look. You can look into a person's eyes and see peace in clear, sparkling eyes, or hurt and sadness can be detected. You need to be very sensitive to your emotions at this time. You can affect your health physically, emotionally, and mentally if you do not deal with sorrow.

Sometimes you think, "What could I have done differently that would have helped or changed the situation?" When you start thinking these thoughts, you have to be careful that guilt doesn't enter. Look at the whole picture. If you were negligent, forgive yourself, and if needed ask others involved to forgive you. If you did all you knew to do, then have a time of grieving, but release it after a period of time. You won't forget immediately, but you must release the negative thoughts that can cause you unnecessary pain and harmful side effects.

If it is something that you can share, talk to family or friends, or find someone that you know you can trust. If you don't want to share your pain with them and you can't overcome the emotions by yourself, seek counsel. You do not need to feel as though you have to carry it alone. But if you feel you need to handle it by yourself, know that you are not alone; Jesus is with you. He loves you, and the Holy Spirit of God is your comforter. Allow God's Holy Spirit to comfort, sustain, and give you His peace. There is nothing wrong with laughter and having joy when you are suffering. Laughter and joy help bring healing.

It may feel like you are in a tunnel where the lights have been turned off and you can't see the end right now. Things will not be the same, but if you have a healthy time of grieving and get peace in your situation, you can go on with life and find happiness. There *is* light at the end of the tunnel. There *is* hope where there seems to be no future. There *will* be rainbows in your sky again. Let the presence of the Lord fill you up to overflowing. You say, "But I can't feel Him right now." Don't worry, He will never leave you nor forsake you. (See Hebrews 13:5, KJV.) Just keep your eyes on Him, do your part, then trust Him to bring you all the way through to your place of joy.

> Do not sorrow, for the joy of the LORD is your strength.
>
> —Nehemiah 8: 10, NKJV

JOY

"Though now you do not see [Jesus], yet believing, you rejoice with joy inexpressible and full of glory" (1 Pet. 1:8, NKJV). What a statement! You have access to the wonderful presence of the Holy Spirit of God that brings joy beyond measure, and you can see and feel His awesome glory.

There is a time to pray, but when God's glory rises up in you, it is a time to be silent and bask in His presence. In His presence, joy, healing, and restoration comes. Words cannot describe the feeling.

In addition to the healing and blessings you may feel, you have to be quiet so that you can hear Him speak to your spirit and because the experience is so awesome there is nothing you can say. Your words seem so inadequate. You just sit, soak in His presence, and receive from Him. You can do nothing to earn it; you just love and worship Him.

You have likely heard people make the statement; "They are such a joy to my heart." You get pleasure from someone bringing joy into your life. When you take time to touch someone, you bring joy to their life and touch their heart. Can you imagine how much more you bring joy to the heart of God when you love and worship Him?

The Bible tells us of joy in the world when the Christ child was born. (See Luke 2:10–14.) Because of His birth, we experience joy, knowing that through Jesus we have salvation. The Bible speaks of joy in heaven over one repenting sinner. (See Luke 15:7.)

A mother's heart is full of joy when her children are born. She enjoys watching them grow and finds pleasure in their accomplishments. It is a joy to be sitting around the dinner table with the family, partaking of a meal, and sharing the events of the day. This time of day is one of my favorite memories, with everyone laughing and sharing. I feel that it brings the family closer together. You may enjoy watching good television programs or movies together. You must have a sharing time of some type as an outlet for your emotions to bring you into tight family unity.

When I was growing up, my family shared musical interests. My uncles, aunts, cousins, family, and friends would get together occasionally and play the guitar, fiddle, harmonica, banjo, etc., and sing. We had a great time!

If you have been negligent in your family sharing time, remember to make a special effort to have good, joyful memories for them to share. When your children are adults, they will share their childhood memories with family and friends.

There is much happiness when good things happen to you, but there is joy in the Lord for you. You can walk in this joy. You can have a song in your heart. Even when hard times come, the joy can still be there if you know that you have a God that loves and cares about you. You will never achieve the ultimate place—there will always be another level to go—but there will not always be hard times. There are great places of blessing as you walk with the Lord, you are faithful, and you endure to the end.

To achieve a high place in finances, you may need to be prepared in order to learn how to handle the finances when they come. If you have not been prepared, you may not know how to keep the blessing. I have seen men work their adult life to build a successful business, only to turn it over to their children, who did not respect their parents' work and instead squandered the business away. This is not always the case. Some children mature and learn, and they take the business higher than the parent did. But there are others that, instead of working to make the business go higher or stay at the level it was, spend without rebuilding. This can lead to destruction. Keep a watchful eye on the place of blessing God has brought you to so that you do not squander His gifts away. Stay tuned to His spirit so that He can lead you to a higher place of blessing.

What a joy it is when you know you have been faithful, and you see the fruit of your labor and commitment. Your household is in much better order, you have become a more mature person, and your outlook on life in general has changed. You are now ready to walk in the blessing of the fruit of your labor with your head held high, a smile on your face, and the joy of the Lord radiating from your very being.

What happens when the joy leaves?

I don't think your joy actually leaves. God's presence is always there. He never leaves you, but sometimes you walk away from Him or neglect to communicate with your heavenly Father. This can cause loneliness or a sense of emptiness. However, somewhere down deep inside, there is joy just waiting to be released—to rise up and bring laughter into your life.

When things keep happening, you may be afraid to hope any more. You may fear that the hope will be snatched away on the brink of your blessing, so you keep joy suppressed and will only let it rise and come to the surface when you see results. I understand this, but don't let hope die. No hope and no vision bring feelings of boredom, sadness, despair, or depression.

If you have health problems and your active lifestyle has been hampered, you will likely start feeling bored. Keep your eyes on Jesus. He is your waymaker where there is no way. He makes a path where the weeds in your life seem to have grown beyond your ability to pull them out or mow them down. He brings clear skies in your storm.

If you have lost a loved one, you will never forget them, but you have to deal with your sorrow. Even though it seems all hope is gone, joy will return. You have to look at your surroundings and get your emotions under control. Do not suppress your emotions; they will only arise again for you to deal with at a later time. Ask Jesus to heal your broken heart or the broken places in your life. Then let His love surround you and give you His peace. Get your focus on the reality of what is going on around you as you let His love flow through you to help you deal with your circumstances and situations.

If your children are bringing heartbreak into your life, always stand with them. No one else will stand with them and emotionally support them like you will. Let them know that you love them, even if they are a prodigal son or daughter. Let them know that you, as their parent, will always be standing, waiting with open arms to receive them in love—back to the Father's house. (See Luke 15:11–20.) Let them know that God loves them, but it is very important that they know without a doubt that they have parents that love them with a pure, unconditional love and want the best for them.

The Lord showed my husband one time that there are five ways God desires to bless you:

1. Spiritually: alive in the Spirit, so as to be in tune with Him, in unity and one accord with His mighty Holy Spirit

2. Physically: strong and healthy

3. Mentally: alert and clear mind, godly thoughts

4. Emotionally: morally straight, healthy nervous system

5. Financially: when all the above steps are in place and functioning, then the way is cleared and open for God to deliver financial blessings

We would all like to be blessed financially, but if you have not dealt with your inner problems, you may not be able to be good stewards when the finances come. God wants you to be spiritually, physically, mentally, and emotionally well. Then when the blessings come, you won't blow it all away. You will be mature and trained to handle the blessings. I don't mean that you won't get blessed in this way until the other areas in your life are totally healed. You may always be dealing with something, but as you walk down your path to wellness and wholeness in these areas, you have learned how to walk through the battles and not have a defeated attitude.

When you have overcome the defeated attitude and get your focus on Jesus, you will start feeling your own abilities returning and know that through Christ, you can do all things. (See Philippians 4:13, KJV.) You can be the person God wants you to be. You can look after your family in peace and not in stress. You can walk through the storms of life with a knowing in your heart that you will get through. Philippians 4:19 says, "And it is he who will supply all your needs from his riches in glory, because of what Christ Jesus has done for us." Not your riches, but His riches!

Joy arises again when your relationship is fulfilled in the Lord. It is manifest in all its glory when you see your home in order and your family happy and healthy, with their lives in control and with a personal relationship with Jesus.

Stay encouraged. Life is full of wonderful, exciting things if you will keep your focus in the right place and your heart and mind open to the goodness life has in store for you. After all is well and your skies are blue again, joy will rise up, and you will have a song in your heart and a smile on your face. Then when the scoffers come or the negative report is sent your way, you will know without a doubt that there is hope. And joy is a part of your life again!

> That the genuineness of your faith, being much more precious than gold that perishes, though it is tested by fire, may be found to praise, honor and glory at the revelation of Jesus Christ, whom having not seen you love. Though now you do not see Him, yet believing, you rejoice with joy inexpressible and full of glory.
>
> —1 Peter 1:7–8, NKJV

> Let all those who seek You rejoice and be glad in You; Let such as love Your salvation say continually, "The Lord be magnified!"
>
> —Psalm 40:16, NKJV

LOVE

> For God loved the world so much that he gave his only Son so that anyone who believes in him shall not perish but have eternal life.
>
> —John 3:16

Love conquers all—an easy and wonderful emotion. It is so wonderful to know that someone truly loves you, but it is usually someone close to you that hurts you the most. You can fluff off rebuffs or rejections from strangers, but the real pain you have to learn to conquer and get victory over usually comes from someone close to you.

There is a thing that is called "smothering with love." Sometimes a person just simply loves someone so much that they love to show them. But if it is not purely motivated, it could become a selfish, controlling emotion.

Then there are people that can't do enough for another. Some are service motivated, and that is good. They love to do things with no strings attached because they love serving people. But there is a selfish motive that can come in if a person is not careful. They may become motivated by the wrong kind of love. Their intentions are to build their own ego and support other self-centered motives instead of acting out of pure love. How many times have you seen a person kiss someone and say, "I love you," but eventually they get around to asking for favors? Is this true love from the heart, or is this just a selfish motivation? If it is for selfish reasons, when they don't get their way, you will shortly see them turning away. If the other person thought they were their friend, pain and hurt may come. In this type of situation, you have to be mature and not put up walls to protect your feelings. You may need to ask forgiveness for letting wrong thoughts and feelings come in, then give your heart and emotions to Jesus. Look beyond the hurt to find someone who is genuinely trying to reach out with love from a pure heart. True love is a love without demands. It is giving your time and energy to family or someone hurting who needs your help and encouragement, or it might be just having a great time together. Speak positive things into the lives of your friends and family. Encourage them and let them know how wonderful they are and how much they mean to you.

Tell them often that you love them, and show them the kind of love that is pure and given unselfishly.

> "As the Father loved Me, I also have loved you; abide in My love. "If you keep My commandments, you will abide in My love, just as I have kept My Father's commandments and abide in His love. "These things I have spoken to you, that My joy may remain in you, and that your joy may be full. "This is my commandment, that you love one another as I have loved you.
>
> —John 15:9–12, NKJV

DISAPPOINTMENT

There have been times in my life when I have had to deal with disappointment. It is not often an easy emotion to deal with. Perhaps you've made plans that may have seemed frivolous to others, but you have your heart set on something. You may have made extensive preparation, but for some reason, finances didn't come through or illness happened. If you had to postpone or forget your plans—whatever the reason—it is hard to deal with if you really had your heart set on it.

One time we were planning a trip. We had taken vacation leave from work and expected finances to be available before we left. We were making a trip to a ministry crusade and then going on to another city to visit my family, including my sister, who was dying of cancer. I felt it was going to be a fun trip, but also a very important and needed one.

It came to a day or so before departure time and the expected money had not come. I started getting upset and couldn't understand why God wouldn't allow us to take this trip. I'm sure everyone could have gotten along without me, but my heart had such a desire to go. All plans were made; we were just waiting for the money. I complained, "I don't understand." At the last minute the money we expected did come in, and I was so happy. I did not have to make such a fuss, but the emotion of disappointment is a strong one, especially if other feelings are involved.

God always does what He promises, but you need to make sure that you have included Him in your plans—especially if you expect Him to provide the money. We went to the crusade, visited my sister (she died only a couple weeks after that visit), and saw other family members, too.

Let God get involved in your life and decisions. God is good, and He loves you very much. He cares about your financial needs, but He will also get very involved in your emotional needs. Your disappointment can turn to joy, your sadness to gladness, and your frown will change to a happy smile!

Chapter 15

ENCOURAGEMENT AND GOD'S CARE

DOES GOD CARE?

MOST OF THE TIME, YOU HAVE STRONG FAITH AND ARE A staunch believer in God and His promises. But when you keep getting hit emotionally, financially, or physically—over and over again, month after month—with one thing after the other, it is easy to begin questioning if God really cares about you. You know without a doubt that God is real, but in difficult times you may start thinking, "I know He is real, but does He care about me and what happens to me?" In your heart you know without a doubt that He loves you and is taking care of you, but still that thought will sometimes enter your mind. You may even start thinking you have blown it.

No, God doesn't treat you like that. He loves you no matter what. Most of the time when you are being hit hard with situations, you really haven't done anything wrong. You just start wearing down physically, mentally, and emotionally, which makes you start looking for something you may have done to cause it or start wondering if God does care. If you dwell on it too much by focusing on your situation, you could convince yourself that He doesn't really care. These times are when it is absolutely necessary to keep your eyes on Jesus, not on your circumstances.

The Bible tells the story in the sixth chapter of Second Kings. It goes something like this:

Once when the king of Syria was at war with Israel, he said to his officers. "Which of you is the traitor?" "It's not us, sir," one of the officers replied. "Elisha, the prophet, tells the king of Israel even the words you speak in the privacy of your bedroom!" The king told them to go and find him. They came back and reported where he was. So one night the king of Syria sent a great army with many chariots and horses to surround the city. When the prophet's servant got up early the next morning and went outside, there were troops, horses, and chariots everywhere. "Alas, my master, what shall we do now?" he cried out to Elisha. "Don't be afraid!" Elisha told him. "For our army is bigger than theirs!" Then Elisha prayed, "Lord, open his eyes and let him see!" And the Lord opened the young man's eyes so that he could see horses of fire and chariots of fire everywhere upon the mountain!

—2 Kings 6:8, 11–17, author's paraphrase

Yes, God cares about you. Sometimes He is working things out in your life that may delay His intervention, like checking your obedience or moving behind the scenes to bring things to pass in the now. But one thing is for sure: He loves you and cares about you. If you take the time to stop and think about it, you can probably name numerous times that you positively knew that He intervened on your behalf—and there's no telling how many times He intervened when you didn't even know about it. If He does allow situations, it is to bring about change in your life for your well-being and for the sake of your place in eternity. Jesus says in Matthew 11:28, "Come to me and I will give you rest—all of you who work so hard beneath a heavy yoke." That means you, too!

At different times in my life, I would know of someone in need, and I would take food from my pantry to help them.

It didn't seem like much at the time. However, I was at a meeting one night, and a man of God spoke a word from the Lord over me concerning those gifts. The following is an excerpt from that word:

> For the Lord has made us. Your walk has been a struggle because God has given you a heart to care for other people. You've been a minister to intercede, sent to hold up the hands of people [whose] lives were destroyed. God sent you to minister and to pour in the healing oil of God. The Lord said He's going to increase to you greater anointing and going to increase to you a greater walk with God. It's because you haven't been selfish of your call or selfish of what it was that God gave to you. You took of your substance, both natural and spiritual, and you gave it to those that were in need. The Lord said this is the day that you shall not go without the things that I have for you. For as you've sowed into the lives of others and have become an intercessor to those with great needs spiritually as well as physically, this shall be a day that you shall reap life and life more abundantly.

Stay encouraged. God sees what you do, and even though what you do may seem small to you, God sees your faithfulness. Say this prayer:

> *When the storms of life try to overtake me and my boat of safety and security is rocking to and fro, Lord of the wind and waves, rescue me. When reports of waves of problems or sickness are heading my way, Lord of the wind and waves, don't let them overtake me, but calm my storms before the waves wash over me and tumble me about. My faith and trust are in*

*You. I know You are the master of the storms of my
life. Keep me safe under Your wings of protection.
Though I may walk through storms in life, I will not
fear, for I know that You are with me. You have my
life in control, and through You my storm will calm
and I will know peace and security. Jesus, You are
Lord of the wind and waves!"*

Yes, God does care about you!

GOOD NEWS

I reflect sometimes on my childhood and think how, as
wonderful as things are today, children in this generation
are missing out on some of the experiences we had when we
were growing up, such as going to the field near the house
and picking wild huckleberries, then bringing the berries
home for mom to cook huckleberry pie. We called it huckleberry pie, but she really just cooked the berries in a lot of
juice and added dumplings.

I grew up in Florida. We had orange, grapefruit, and
tangerine trees to eat and mango and guava trees to climb to
reach their delicious fruit. You may have grown up in an area
where pecan, peach, pear, cherry, or apple trees grew. There
aren't many homes anymore that have fruit trees growing
in the yard. In a lot of situations, children don't have the
blessing of shady yards with trees to play in. They have to
deal with street violence and coming home to an empty
house. Life requires, in most cases, for both parents to work
outside the home.

Life seemed much simpler then. We were building character and stability as a heritage for our children, which in
the end brings character and stability to our nation. We must

keep the roots of our heritage. Whether you grew up in the city or country, no matter how insecure the world outside appears to be, you have stabilizing, secure memories that the children of your future will inherit—a loving and caring atmosphere of home.

I can remember going to my grandmother's when I was very young. She would sit in a rocking chair and sing to me. The memory of the moment and her special touch has lasted all these years.

Sometimes the cares of life keep you distracted, but keep in mind: today's cares may be temporary, but your influence on your family will last forever. I am sharing this with you so that you can think about the things that you do or have done with your children and grandchildren that may be some of the highlights in their life with you. Take this to heart and do everything you can to give them loving, happy memories of you—things that will give them a secure childhood now and memories they can share with their families for generations to come.

It may not have always been easy committing to being like Jesus, but it is a joy knowing that through it all you can overcome. After you have accepted Jesus as your Savior and you have committed to all He asks of you, there is good news. God loves you! Jesus died for you! By His stripes you are healed! The Holy Spirit is here to teach and guide you! His goodness and unfailing kindness shall be with you all your life! And afterwards you will live with Him forever in His home! (See John 3:16; 1 Peter 2:24; 1 Corinthians 2:13; 1 John 2:27; Psalm 23:6; John 14:3.)

YOU WILL GET TO THE OTHER SIDE

I hope you have enjoyed the experiences I have shared with you, those that I have acquired along the way while walking the walk in a real world. I hope as you read this little book, you began to understand what is transpiring in your life and have a greater desire to go further in your walk with the Lord.

The Holy Spirit draws you to give your heart to Jesus in salvation, but the Bible also encourages us in Psalms 119:2, "Happy are all who search for God, and always do his will." He wants to take you into a deep, closer experience in His presence. Not everyone is willing to pay the price, so He is looking for people that will say, "I am willing, Lord." What an honor that God can look at you and see your willingness. What a joy to be drawn into His presence to grow and be taught by His Holy Spirit.

As you climb your mountains and experience joy and blessings, or cross your valley of despair, keep your eyes on Jesus and hold on to His promises. With perseverance and trusting God, although you may get there with scars, you will get to the other side.

> But he knows every detail of what is happening to me;
> and when he has examined me, he will pronounce me
> completely innocent—as pure as solid gold!
> —Job 23:10

COMMITMENT

NOW THAT YOU HAVE READ MY LITTLE BOOK, *Walking the Walk in a Real World*, I would like to ask you, where are you in your relationship with the Lord? Have you accepted Jesus as your Savior? Is He Lord of your life? Jesus loves you so much that He came to Earth to die for you. If you are unhappy and want a change in your life, all you have to do is ask Jesus to forgive your sins and then ask Him to come into your life and be Lord. Tell Him you are tired of trying it your way and want a change. Believe that He died on the cross and shed His blood to pay the price for your sins and then He rose again. Know that after you have committed your life to Him, you can live with Him in heaven throughout all eternity. Just ask! He loves you and is waiting for you to invite Him in to be your Lord and Savior.

If you have already accepted Jesus as your Savior, then let the Holy Spirit lead you into a deeper relationship and commitment to Him. When you go to your place of prayer and are alone with the Lord, as you are praising and worshiping Him and you feel His presence, make an effort to lay down your hindering thoughts and put them aside as they try to enter your mind. Tell Him how much you love Him, that you desire His presence, and that He is welcome in your life. Love Him and worship Him as He draws near. In His presence, there is healing for your hurts and your broken heart, and there is peace from all your problems. Whatever situation you have encountered in life, put them all aside and dwell on His presence. As you enter into the holy presence of God, it is an awesome place. The God of all creation is drawing near to you, and as you worship Him, you will draw near to Him. Leave all your cares behind and receive all that He has for you. Let His presence touch your life, and you will be a changed person because of Him.

God loves you and desires that you walk in total commitment of your life to Him so that you can have a better quality life and help others along the way that need you to reach out a loving hand to touch them with God's love.

NOTES

Chapter 13

LOVE, MAINTENANCE, AND SPIRITUAL GROWTH

1. Inez Alexander, letter to the editor, *Naples Daily News*, December 24, 1971.

Bob and Flash (our faithful German shepherd dog)
after returning home from the hospital.